A Mother's Words ...

Beyond the Grave

A Mother's Words ...
Beyond the Grave

*Transforming
Anger into Forgiveness
&
Pain into Peace*

Melinda A. Angstadt

Order this book online at www.trafford.com/07-0352
or email orders@trafford.com

Most Trafford titles are also available at major online book retailers.

Note for Librarians: A cataloguing record for this book is available from Library
and Archives Canada at www.collectionscanada.ca/amicus/index-e.html

Printed in Victoria, BC, Canada.

ISBN: 978-1-4251-1945-4

*We at Trafford believe that it is the responsibility of us all, as both individuals
and corporations, to make choices that are environmentally and socially sound.
You, in turn, are supporting this responsible conduct each time you purchase a
Trafford book, or make use of our publishing services. To find out how you are
helping, please visit www.trafford.com/responsiblepublishing.html*

*Our mission is to efficiently provide the world's finest, most comprehensive
book publishing service, enabling every author to experience success.
To find out how to publish your book, your way, and have it available
worldwide, visit us online at www.trafford.com/10510*

www.trafford.com

North America & international
toll-free: 1 888 232 4444 (USA & Canada)
phone: 250 383 6864 ♦ fax: 250 383 6804
email: info@trafford.com

The United Kingdom & Europe
phone: +44 (0)1865 722 113 ♦ local rate: 0845 230 9601
facsimile: +44 (0)1865 722 868 ♦ email: info.uk@trafford.com

10 9 8 7 6 5 4 3 2

In honor of my mother,

Judith S. Michrina,

who walked her path Home,

and then,

came back to tell all about the journey.

Acknowledgements

I am deeply grateful to the many people
who have helped
make this book possible:

My longtime friend, Sue Johnson,
for her patience while I grew into this work, and her
perseverance in reading and re-reading the manuscript.
Thank you for sharing your life with me.

My sister, Shelly Michrina,
for her beautiful Butterfly Story,
and for standing beside me
as I searched for my purpose in this lifetime.

My sister, Debbie Michrina,
for answering the phone that very first day,
and for being so understanding and supportive
through the process of hearing these messages.

My husband, Larry Angstadt,
for allowing me the space to go through so many changes,
and for still loving me
even though I am no longer the girl he married.

My Reiki Master and "sister," Susan Drey,
for introducing me to the spiritual world,
and for guiding me toward a new life.

My angel with crooked wings, Rev. Joan Wolfe,
for having the confidence in me that I lacked for myself,
and for pushing me out of the nest
even though I thought I would never be able to fly.

My best friend, Janice Hoffmaster,
who listened and listened and listened some more,
through tears and laughter, smiles and hugs,
and lots of chili cheese nachos.
Thank you for being my "bestest" friend forever.

My friend, Harriet Levy,
for being my cheerleader,
and for her constant encouragement
during the process of publishing this book.

My proofreaders,
Beccie, Ellen, and Joan,
for taking time out of their busy schedules
to proofread the final book copy.

My editor, Susan Kern,
for gently nurturing and caring for "my baby."

My soul friend and colleague, Rev. Kenneth White,
for always lifting my soul to its highest.

My teacher and friend, Rev. Hannelore Goodwin,
for loving me through the trials of my past,
for giving me the tools of my future,
and for being a Light upon this earth.

All the angels and guides,
who came and spoke so freely about
Truth, Light, and Love.

And most of all my parents,
Daniel and Judith Michrina,
for walking a very difficult path in this lifetime,
all so that I could find out who I really was.

Contents

Foreword

As I write this, I am sitting in a beautiful Bed and Breakfast in Wellsboro, Pennsylvania. A few days in the mountain air always renews my soul. I have just finished reading *A Mother's Words ... Beyond the Grave*, and as I place it on the table next to me I notice a unique sensation wash over me as if every cell in my body is resonating at a new vibration, softly whispering, "Remember, remember the wisdom." Tears of joy are rolling down my face as I realize that this book has brought me to a greater understanding of what walking in Divine Faith truly means.

Each part of this book is a journey into the writer's soul that allows us to travel back and forward within our own souls. Each line is a constant reminder of the tenacity of the soul's desire to learn, grow and survive. I know that for me it is not a once and done kind of read, but a form of daily mediation. I love being able to pull it off of the shelf on occasion and open it randomly to a page or two that will speak softly to the unconscious, amazed at how the vibrations of the words deeply touch me inside! Therein lays the gift to the reader!

This is a book for the novice seeker as well as the experienced spiritual teacher, as each part is broken down into lessons that prepare readers for their own experience. Each and every reader will derive from its words a unique experience unto themselves based on what their life has brought them to date.

Part One describes the experience and energy of a child, a little warrior seeking acceptance and love under the harshest conditions of the family tribe.

Part Two explains the pain of growth and enlightenment. It reminds us all of our ability to commune with spirit and prepares us for our own journey of awakening.

Part Three becomes forms of chants and affirmations for the reader. This is especially useful; I found myself repeating some of the messages throughout the course of my day. In the stillness of perceptual shift, it allows the reader to begin to understand why things happen to us in this lifetime.

It is clear that Melinda has taken intense Karmic debt and turned it into a tool for growth and renewal that is sure to touch the very depth of the reader's soul. She has made a difference in the lives of so many people as this book was manifesting within her. I can only begin to imagine the lessons it will invoke in each of its readers as the energy of each word brings a new dawn.

I am truly convinced as long as the world has people like Melinda in it, there will always be hope and faith, contributing to a brighter, more peaceful understanding of the future. As her teacher, friend, and spiritual sister, she has reminded me of what it feels like to let my heart sing with joy and triumph.

It is with great admiration that I, and I am sure you, embrace this wonderful book and use it to learn even more about what is really important in our lives.

Susan R. Drey
Executive Director,
Pennsylvania Center for Intuitive Studies

Preface

There are many things I can say that I have been in my life. I've been a jack-of-all-trades, and a master of some; yet I have always felt that I was destined to do something of great importance. At age forty-five, being a mother of five and a grandmother of four, I still joked about not knowing what I wanted to be when I grew up. The sad truth was I really didn't know.

I have been able to be a stay-at-home mom for the past twenty years, raising my children and becoming a professional volunteer. I enjoyed volunteering my time, and was one of the few mothers who did not work at least part-time. Since housework has never been high on my importance list, I've always had time to help with the parties at school, chaperone the field trips, assist with the concerts, be a Cub Scout den leader, a Sunday School teacher, and the list goes on and on.

Understand that this is the life I chose, and I will never regret it. Being a full-time mom is one of the most challenging and rewarding jobs you can ever undertake. It's 24-7, with no pay and few benefits, except for all the hugs (which is why I kept the job for so many years). My life has always been busy and fulfilling, but there was always something missing.

Through nothing less than a miracle—what was missing—was found. Suddenly I realized that all the voices in my head were not the ramblings of my own lonesome mind, but the voices of the Angelic Realm. And the voices told me exactly what I had always known in my heart—there was more!

I welcome you and invite you to open your mind and heart as you meet the voices of the Angelic Realm.

Introduction

This is a story of healing, of ultimate love, and especially of forgiveness; a story that could not be written until after the death of my mother. It is remarkable that the relationship we could not have in life has been easily accomplished after her death. I feel closer to her now than ever before. It is a closeness that could not be achieved while she was alive.

This is our story.

Mom passed over after a long and agonizing battle with cancer. She had beaten it once before, but this time the malignancy ravaged her body to the point where conventional medicine ended and prayers began. The months prior to her diagnosis had been the breaking point in our relationship, which was now damaged beyond repair. Even as she told me of the cancer, I was unable to summon the feelings that should have been there. I was completely devoid of emotion. I just did not care. Such thoughts had never before entered my mind, but the anger that was in my heart had so completely overshadowed what had once been love, I was lost in a sea of apathy.

As the months went by and she endured the rounds of chemotherapy, I kept informed of her progress but did not offer to help her in any way. It was not that I hated her; I had just come to the point where she didn't matter to me anymore. It was as if she had been a stranger all my life. She had never been there for me, and now by a twist of fate, I would not be there for her. There was no revenge in what I was doing. There was no hatred and no guilt. There was nothing.

As the end came closer, she was hospitalized with a deadly infection and I could no longer avoid visiting her. Not knowing what to say, I was terrified to be alone with her. We were strangers. Despite these feelings, I was there to feed her and to sit with her as the morphine caused her mind to slip into delusions. The minute by minute tasks included reassuring her that she had her wallet, that chickens were not cooking in the cabinet of the Intensive Care Unit, and that the pink bunny she saw dancing on her dinner tray was not really there. It was heart breaking to watch my mother in this state of mind. The numbness began to lift, leaving me with new feelings of compassion and caring.

What she went through should have killed her, but she had always been a survivor. She had spent almost three weeks in the hospital incoherent or comatose when one day suddenly, she recovered. It was miraculous to see her sitting up in bed, eating, and talking—or should I say bitching. This was wrong—and that wasn't right—and where was everyone to help her? As I watched and listened, I sadly realized that the old Mom was back. Nothing had—or ever would—change. How could I have been so foolish as to let her back into my heart? It was at this moment that the heart which had begun to soften, turned to stone.

Within the day, however, we realized that this had not been a miracle. She was merely a light bulb which burned brightly just before it blew out. She sank into a deep, coma-like state waiting to die. Those last days were the most difficult of all. She could not speak and she did not open her eyes, but she was listening; her mind alert within a dying body.

Days went by and even the doctors could not understand why she had not let go. This resulted in an exhausting vigil for all of us. It was as if she were searching for absolution, believing in an eternal life with God, but terrified of going to hell. We were with her when the end finally came; she breathed her last breath, and the agony was over. It was done, and I had been the good dutiful daughter right to the end.

I thought it was over; that my existence could all of a sudden become all that it had not been. The evil in my life was gone, and so I assumed that all the pain would be gone also. But a lifetime of pain cannot be erased in the blink of an eye. My mother was gone; nevertheless, the anguish which was our life was right where we had left it. It was still in my heart, and without releasing the pain, my life was to continue just as it had always been.

I had my wish: my mother was gone, but now I was trapped in an unending hurt. The time for forgiveness and friendship had been forfeited, and I felt as if my life would be lost forever.

I turned to the only One I knew would listen. I began to pray for peace and healing in my life, and in exchange I vowed that I would become a messenger of God's Word. Sitting by my altar at home I made this request and promise for months, not knowing exactly why, but knowing that it was what I needed to do.

And then came the day when she stood by my computer. I did not see her, nor did I know that it was she; but I felt the presence of someone, and I knew exactly what I was to do. I sat and I listened. I heard nothing, but my fingers flew over the keyboard as if they had a life of their own. Although the typing was completely incoherent, I knew that there was an important message somewhere within all the mixed-up letters.

As my fingers finally stilled, words began to form in my mind. I was not sure what was going on. Where were the words coming from? Were they the fantasies of my own mind? How could I be hearing voices within my own head? As the questions raged, all I could do was type furiously. Amid my own confusion came clearly the words ... *"this is your mother."* She spoke of the past and of the future. She explained about all the hurt that was in my heart, and she apologized for having caused it. It was not my own mind talking. It *was* my mother. Two lifetimes of torment—hers and mine—have been erased by the gift which was given to us.

This is a book of messages from my mother and the Angelic Realm. I have met many angels: Char is the Goddess of Love, Damon the Angel of Soothing Music, and Daniel is my guardian angel. Each has come into my life, and melted the icicle that once covered my heart.

I know my mother for the first time in my life, and she is not who I thought she was. Her life was her path, just as my life is mine. Understanding the way of the path has brought clarity to my life, and it can bring it to your life also. The messages contained in this book are from the Angelic Realm. God, Himself, has come to speak to me. All their words are here not only for me, but for you as well.

There are so many of you who have had hurtful and abusive relationships with your loved ones. Not knowing what to do with all the anger and pain can make life a living hell. The angels are here to help! Your heart and your life will be healed through their words.

Part One is the story of my life. In order for you to understand the importance of the relationship I now have with my mother, you must understand the dysfunction that surrounded me as a child, and how it ultimately affected every part of my adult life.

Part Two contains the first month of messages. These words are directed toward the healing of my life. It was necessary for me to move through my own pain before I would be able to clearly hear the messages that were to be sent for you. These messages bear the innermost thoughts of my mother, the Angelic Realm, and me.

Part Three begins your journey. On this day the messages changed. They were no longer directed to me, but were sent for you. These are the messages that will heal your life. Take them to heart, live them, and you will know unending peace. It will take work to transform your pain, but the peace that is on the other side is your reward.

Part Four offers in-depth insight into nuances of the mind and the soul, as well as presenting practical suggestions for releasing the pain and gaining the peace which you are seeking.

Angels are not known for their grammar skills, and so they don't always speak in complete sentences. If you are well-educated in the English language, try not to let their speaking style distract you from hearing what is being said. Distraction is a trick of the mind.

You will also find lots of repetition. It is the angelic way of teaching. Only in repetition will we be able to fully learn and remember their messages. I would suggest that you read them just as I received them. Read one message a day and then take those teachings out into your world. You may not always succeed in living them, but practice is the way to mastery.

This is not a book to read and place on the shelf—never to be picked up again. Read and re-read the messages until they become part of your existence. They will become your path to God and to knowing yourself as you have never known your Self before. Sit back, put your feet up, and enjoy the journey. You will not be alone!

PART ONE

The Days of Childhood
& Beyond

**The Truth in you remains radiant as a star, as
pure as Light, as innocent as love itself.**

A Course In Miracles

The Days of Childhood
& Beyond

My Mother's Past

My mother was an only child, born to a mother who spent her life trying to project perfection to the outside world. She kept her house meticulously clean, dressed like a perfect lady, and tried in vain to make her daughter the perfect child. There had never been much love within that house, and my mother spent most of her childhood in her room spinning fantasies in her young mind.

When I was born, the little bit of love my mother had been shown was yanked away and given to me. I believe in my grandmother's eyes, I was a new chance for her to create perfection. As a child, I was very close to my grandmother, and I could never understand the animosity that my mother had for her. It was not until I was an adult that I realized why my mother was so jealous of my relationship with my grandmother. It was because I had replaced her in her mother's heart.

A child will live and learn through the emotions of its parents. And so a child raised in pain, abuse, and fear will raise her own children in the same pain, abuse, and fear, for it is the only thing she knows.

My Mother Speaks

Weeks have passed since I wrote about my mother's childhood. It has been an overwhelming emotional task to even think about putting the stories of my own childhood into words. Unlike most children, my two sisters and I remember very little of our young lives. Perhaps this is a survival mechanism—or possibly it is just that there was not much to remember. The majority of our memories are ones that are better left lying in the dust, hidden under an old carpet.

The angels have repeatedly told me that in order for this book to be helpful to others, I must tell all who read it about my life and my relationship with my mother. Many of you have come to this book because of hurt that you have suffered throughout your life. In order for you to understand the healing that the angels have brought to me through their messages, you must first know the disgust that I felt for my own mother.

A lack of knowing the proper way to speak about my mother has brought me to this point. The questions are daunting. Do I want to place my past in the open for all to see? Why would I ever want to do this? How do I tell the story without damaging my mother? I have been re-united with her only through these messages, and I am afraid of hurting her feelings or making her angry. I have been unable to sit and write because of these doubts.

And then one day, the answer came straight from my mother. She has been in my heart, and knows the turmoil that I have been enduring. She will start; she will write the words to tell all of my past.

These are the words she spoke to me.

This is as it was, and this is what you shall write. Your life has been a series of tragedies, and you have risen above each and become stronger.

I had such high hopes for my first child. I had hoped that she would become all I had not been; I had hoped that she could be everything I could not. These were my dreams, and in those dreams I hoped to heal my own childhood.

When you were born, I was so happy. You were so precious. You were not as beautiful as I expected, but you were all mine. You were mine, and no one could take this away from me. You were my chance to do something good with my life.

As you grew and your sisters were born, your father and I drifted apart. He began drinking and stopped coming home after work. Life was becoming unbearable. I was left alone most nights, and I feared that he was with another woman. Alone in the cold in the middle of nowhere with three little girls, I reflected upon my life. I could see that my adult life was to be as loveless as my childhood. It was a devastating fact which would change the rest of my—and more importantly—your life. As I sat with the cats, the dirty diapers, and the loneliness, I knew that all was to continue just as it was. I would not be a success in adult life any more than I had been in childhood. This is who I was—a failure—unable to please my parents, and now unable to keep a husband.

There came a day when the end was imminent. And then the words, "I need to find myself," which were spoken by your father. He was not sure that he wanted to be a father and husband anymore. Fine time to wonder about this—ten years and three children into the marriage. But wimp that I was, I washed his clothes, packed his bags, and wished him well—all the time dying inside.

I had never been alone. I had lived with my parents until I entered the Air Force, and then I married your father. There had always been someone there to take care of me. Never had I needed to survive on my own. There was only one thing that I could do now. I packed up my girls and moved home with my parents.

In the next few years, there were comings and goings on your father's part. You were moved so many times, depending on whether he was with us or whether he was not. I knew that changing school districts back and forth was difficult for you, but living with my parents was intolerable for me. It was a constant confirmation that I was a failure. And now my precious children were under the same scrutiny I had lived through as a child.

It was more than I could bear. I needed a way out of the pain, a way to forget about everything that was so wrong with my life. I spent days and nights drinking, but my parents never suspected anything. The good thing about living at home was that I really did not have to be the mother, because my mother was taking care of all my children's needs. She always told me she could do a better job anyway.

We finally escaped from the oppression of my parents' home a few years later, but living on our own was more of a shock than I had expected. All of a sudden it was up to me to be the mother, and I was not prepared. Now not only was I heavily into drinking, but I was also addicted to diet pills. The diet pills of the 60s were amphetamines; they were unregulated and I could get as many as I wanted whenever I needed them. No one counted the pills, and no one checked to see if I was due for more. It was just another way to deny my life, and I became hooked.

Then came a time when the booze and pills were no longer an effective way to escape, so I turned to men to boost my self-worth. Leaving you alone to become the mother was the cruelest thing that I could have done to a twelve-year-old. As I rode the buses in search of someone to make me feel loved, you were home making supper and

5

caring for your sisters. You never knew a childhood; you grew up way too fast. As things got worse, you became the mother, and I the wayward child.

This was your life, and I did not understand how I could do this to you, my precious child, but I did not know how to stop it. It was like a train rumbling through the barriers at the end of the station. There was no brake, and I knew that it was going to be a disaster, but I did not have the strength to even try to stop our lives from derailment.

When we moved into the housing project, I figured that it would be a chance for you to fit in—to become just like the rest of the kids. In the project no one had a father and no one had money. No one had fancy clothes and no one had cars. I had hoped that this would be the chance for me to fit in as well. I was blessed with a new job, an old car, and food stamps. Now we were on our way. We would be fine. I would be a success!

The future held no success, however. The pull of the alcohol was too strong, and my own lack of self-esteem made succeeding impossible. As an Extension Service home aide, I began cheating on work time and hiding the car so that no one would know I was actually at home. Making up home visit sheets and not answering the phone became my way of life.

Years of deceit led me deeper and deeper along the path of self-destruction. You cannot believe how deep you can get in the muck when you have nothing in your life that seems good. And now, after years of neglect, I felt my girls were growing into their own persons based on the life that I had given them.

You were the over-achiever—always trying to make things perfect and pretending there was nothing wrong. You studied so hard for school, worked at McDonald's, did all the housework, and took care of your sisters the best that you could. It used to break my heart to watch you come home from school, run to the store to get something

6

for supper, cook, and do a load of laundry, all before you went to work. I knew that this was not the life for a sixteen-year-old, but there was nothing I could do. I was wallowing in the self-pity that was my life.

Debbie went the other way. She was breaking out, doing her own thing, and getting into lots of trouble. Who could blame her? She was just looking for attention and love. There was none at home so she had to strike out to find it elsewhere. Debbie always reminded me of your father, and I think this was the reason I was always angry with her. She was the hardest to love, and I could not understand why. All I knew was that when I looked at her I saw contempt. I treated her so badly. The alcohol and the devastation of my life had clouded my perspective so that I could not see clearly anymore. And now I had lost Debbie. She was gone, never to be my child again—never to be a child again.

My baby, Shelly, was the most important one in my life. She was my last chance. She would be my crowning glory. All would look to me and say, "You are a good mother. Look at Shelly. She is so smart and so pretty." She was my last chance to prove my mothering skills. Instead, she became a pawn for you and Debbie to try and win over to your side, all the time having a neurotic mother pushing her to become the best. Now keep in mind, I was not supporting her to be her best, I just expected her to be it. But after constantly being teased about being a dumb blonde, she became timid, shy, and insecure.

What you are told you are as a child, you will become. You were good, and so you became overly good—too scared to take chances in life. Debbie was told that she was a tramp, and so that is what she became—all the while just looking for love. Shelly was told she was dumb, and so she grew up thinking that she was helpless. Her beauty would have to be her way to survive the cruel world.

This was the way of your life. You grew up in a home

7

filled with anger, hurt, and ridicule. Your life was a series of tragedies, beginning with losing your father and then your mother, and unfortunately, this was only the beginning ...

I brought him into the house; it was my fault, not yours. I knew what he was doing, but I was too afraid that he would leave me. I had an engagement ring and a man. For the first time in so long, there was someone who loved me. I should have protected you, but I could not. I was so afraid of being alone again.

I pushed the feelings of disgust aside because I knew you did not know what was going on. Your body had suffered such anguish that your mind was wiped clean. I knew when you came downstairs you did not know that it had happened. I thought, in my delusional mind, this made it okay.

Then the day came that you got pregnant, and I could no longer look and say that this was not hurting you because you did not know. You were having my fiancés baby. I was devastated, and so I threw him out with the excuse that I found him in bed with a friend of mine. The shame that I felt was almost unbearable, but I took you to the abortion clinic, and lied about your pregnancy. It was done—never to be spoken of again.

What you did not know in reality you must have known in your heart. You entered a state of depression, and became plagued with migraine headaches. The doctor told us that they were caused by test anxiety, but I knew the real reason. And so it did not go away as I had hoped. It was still there taunting me, always making sure I knew just how bad a mother I really was.

I kept this secret to my grave, but it was never a secret to me. Each time I looked into your face I saw his face mocking me, telling me that I was a failure as a mother. I prayed you would never remember, even though part of me wanted you desperately to know. I thank you for keeping this a secret from me when you did remember. Having you confront me with it in life would have been more than I could bear.

The worst thing I did, however, was to drive a wedge between you and your sisters. Life was a competition to see who would get my love. There was only enough love for one, and I made sure that the one who was good received it. In the love department, it was pretty much between you and Shelly because Debbie knew that there was no love there for her. She knew, because I told her. How I could have been so cruel I do not know. It saddens my heart to know all the hurt I have caused.

And now it is time for you to tell your story. I have gotten you started. I have told the worst of the things. Now it is your turn. You must sit and write about your childhood so that all may know the hurt and the anger you felt for me during my life. You must tell so all may know that it is possible to go beyond the suffering of the past.

Sit now and write. Write all that is in your heart. I will be with you. Do not fear that you will hurt my feelings or that I will leave you. I will not. Tell the truth—the whole truth—for in the truth of the past, all will see just how truly miraculous these messages are. Know that you have the strength. Know that the words will come. Know that I am with you.

Now write.

My Past

It is so hard to put into words what I have spent most of my life denying. For the abused child, life is an ever-changing array of emotions. The carefree life that every child hopes for and deserves is buried so deeply below all the pain that it can no longer be found. This is the child's way of coping with the loss, for what can no longer be found can no longer be missed. All hope is gone. Now it is a matter of survival.

I have spent a lifetime trying to convince myself that I neither held my parents responsible for my childhood, nor had any hostility toward them. I tried with all my will to forgive them, but could not. It is only after four decades of anger that the truth has been able to enter my heart: my parents were not perfect, but they had done the best that they could.

It is in knowing my parents were not perfect that I could forgive them for what has passed. It is in understanding they did the best that they could, that I can write about my life. I do not feel I am degrading their memories because they have nothing of which they need to be ashamed. Each did the best that he or she could at the time. Knowing and understanding this has been the key to forgiving and loving them again.

And so I shall remember and write:

I was born the oldest of three girls to parents who had been desperately trying to have a baby. An unplanned surprise, my sister Debbie was born two years later. Shelly was conceived three years after that as a desperate plan to save an already deteriorating marriage.

I remember very little of my father, even though I was eight years old when he left. I never remember being held by him or kissed goodnight. Perhaps the memories would have been too upsetting for such a young child to remember, and so they were buried deep within my soul.

One of the clearest memories that I do have is receiving a letter from him while he was living in Florida. He told of the beautiful fountains in his new home, and said that he could not wait until I could come to see them. I waited for years to see the fountains—and my father—until it became obvious that I would never see either of them. As I grew older, I modified my thinking to be thankful that my father had left me. At least he was gone—never to hurt me again.

The move into my grandparents' home was a great joy! I was very close to my grandmother (we were both Virgos), and it was wonderful to be able to climb into her four-poster bed anytime I wanted. Being the firstborn, I was given the privilege of being my grandmother's favorite grandchild. We would take the bus to market for ten cents, and the lady at the chip stand would give me free potato chips. My grandmother taught me how to sew, and how to spell Mississippi while I was home in bed recovering from meningitis. I got the best from my grandmother, and everyone else got what was left. Of course, at age ten, I didn't see it this way. My grandmother could do no wrong in my eyes.

My mother, I believe, saw this as an ultimate betrayal. I had stolen the love which was meant to be hers. Whenever she was angry with me she would tell me that I was just like her mother—a Virgo—cold, sulking, and judgmental. Even as a child, I could feel the hate she had for her mother, and forever she made sure I knew that I was just like her.

As delighted as I was living with my grandparents, there was another side that was sheer torture. We now lived in an upscale school district, and as we all know, kids can be very cruel. In 1964, there was very little divorce and a father's desertion was almost unheard of, especially in that neighborhood. The years we lived there were some of the happiest and saddest in my life.

It was with great exhilaration that we were able to move out into our own apartment and become a family again. Little did I know of the upheaval that was to follow. Mom had such high hopes for all of us. She thought that it truly was a new beginning—and it was. It was the beginning of the end of my childhood. It was time for me to grow up—fast.

I was old enough to understand my mother had been drinking, but now she did not have to hide it. She was free to drink out in the open without the fear of being caught by her parents. As the drinking became worse, Mom gained weight. A trip to the neighborhood doctor brought home the solution: diet pills. Mom had found a way to get an even bigger high than alcohol.

As she became increasingly addicted, it took more pills to produce the desired effect. Mom would give me a couple bucks; down I would walk to the doctor, and home I would come with more pills. The more pills she used the more erratic the "downer." She would stay up all night, drink, and clean the apartment until the pills wore off. I will never forget waking up to find her dead asleep on her hands and knees; she had been cleaning under the radiator.

As the pills worked their miracle of weight loss, she became very interested in searching for love. So now, between the alcohol and chemical abuse, and working and going out, there was very little time for her to be home. As I had two younger sisters, there was no other choice; I became the mother. I was the one who took care of Shelly when she had a fever. And when I called my mother and asked her to come home, I was the one who was yelled at because the fever had broken, and there was no reason that she needed to be there. This was my life. I was twelve years old.

Twelve years turned into thirteen, then fourteen, and fifteen. I was doing my best to try and hold the family together, but it was clear even to me that I was failing. Debbie was running wild, getting into all kinds of trouble, and Shelly just seemed to be lost, not knowing exactly where to fit in.

Mom had given up the diet pills and her weight now topped 310 pounds. Her best friend was still the vodka, and the weight made it even harder for her to actually take charge of her life. She spent her days and nights sitting in her chair, watching television, fantasizing about the actors on her favorite shows.

She rarely left the house except to drive to the liquor store. Even she must have been embarrassed by her drinking habits, because she knew the location of all the liquor stores in the county. Every day there was a different store. Occasionally, we would stop for dinner at one of the fast food (usually fried chicken) restaurants. We would always eat in the car because Mom was too big to get out and go in. This was where we bonded. This was the time that was ours alone. It is no wonder that to this day food is a comfort and that I, too, am seriously overweight. Food equals love!

Even though my mother did nothing for me, I desperately needed her approval. I spent my teenage years trying to make everything right. I figured that if I kept running in circles saying everything was okay, it would be. I just wanted a normal household with a normal parent, but in our house I was the parent, and it was anything but normal.

One of the most damaging things my mother was responsible for was creating a chasm between my sisters and me. We were always told just how different we were, and how we would never be able to get along because of those differences. Having been placed as the defender of what was right; I got into horrible physical fights with Debbie. My mother would just leave and sit out on the front porch as we beat the crap out of each other. I was the "good" one, and it was my job to make everyone know what the right thing to do was.

Being the good one had its advantage because the good daughter got the love. I could never understand why, but Mom could only ever love one of us at a time. This meant that we were always competing; always trying to be one up on the others. This competition continued through adult life, so the rift was always there. It is what kept us separate as sisters for most our lives.

When I was fifteen, my mother brought her fiancé to the house to live with us. I never knew what was happening to me. Even though I had blocked the abuse out of my conscious mind, the memories were apparently being held deep within my soul because somehow I knew that I needed to get out of that house.

At the very young age of nineteen, I met a man only a year older than myself. Perhaps it was his Navy whites or perhaps it was this unconscious need to escape that made me accept his marriage proposal after only knowing him a few months. What should not have surprised me, but somehow still does, is that the man I married was a sexually addicted alcoholic. Looking back I can see that he, too, was just trying to escape his own demons, as well as his own abusive childhood. We married, had a son, and promptly got divorced. The whole mess took less than two years.

I found single parenting to be not much different than parenting my mother, my sisters, or my ex-husband. I was still the one expected to do it all, and so doing it all became my driving force. For the next two decades, my motto became: if I don't do it—it won't get done! I felt as if I was all alone in my little rowboat stuck in the middle of a storm that raged only within my own mind. Everyone in my life had left me. There was no one on whom I could depend other than myself!

I met a wonderful man five years after my first marriage ended. We married, blending his family of two children with mine, and then adding two more of our own. You would think this would have been my happy ending, but as a mother of five and the wife of a workaholic, I found myself still to be a single parent, still all alone in my own little rowboat, still being able to depend only on myself.

14

Life had not changed much since my childhood. Oh the players changed, and the circumstances changed, but the underlying issues were still the same as twenty-five years earlier. At the core of my very being, I was still just a scared fifteen year old. I was scared of not being good enough, scared of being left, scared of the anger I felt for my abusive parents, and most of all, scared of all the uncomfortable fears which had always clouded my sexual relationships.

Quite suddenly, at age forty-one, I began to remember all that had happened upstairs behind closed doors. Little by little, fragments of memories of the abuse long held locked behind my own mind began to surface like shards of glass pushing through a sheer fabric curtain. I don't know whether it was out of a weird sense of love or a complete sense of repulsion, but I kept these memories a secret from my mother, allowing her to continue to happily live in her own denial of what had happened all those years ago.

The physical mind has an incredible protection mechanism, and mine had safely kept all these disturbing memories carefully hidden until it was time for me to remember. But, as wonderful as remembering turned out to be in the end, the process sent me spiraling into what I can only call a complete physical, mental, and emotional breakdown. There were days where I would lay on the floor curled in the fetal position too paralyzed to move. These, of course, were the bad days. On good days, I was a force to be reckoned with! A Super Mom complete with cape and bullet-reflecting wristbands, I was everywhere, involved in everything, with every child, driving myself steadily into the ground, not even realizing that the driving force behind my life was to be anything other than like my mother.

To be fair, I must tell you that my life had begun to fall apart long before these memories began appearing. I had been in therapy for years trying to reconcile my drive for perfection with my overwhelming sense of unworthiness. It had been a long and complicated process that seemed to be going nowhere. Hence is the reason, I believe, that these memories arose. Remembering was one of the most terrifying and wonderful events in my life, because it was only through remembering that I could begin to forget.

Through the years, my mother's insecurities and neuroses grew. She stayed in her apartment and withdrew into a world of fantasy—a world where she was important and everyone loved her. This world did not include her children or even her grandchildren, and this hurt me very deeply. Even as an adult, I could not depend on her for support of any kind.

She was my mother, and yet she was not someone whom I knew or wanted to know. I no longer cared if what I did pleased her; I no longer wanted to be the good daughter. I had been good and taken care of her all my life, but in a moment it was forgotten. When I did not stay in line I was pushed aside, and either Debbie or Shelly became the object of her affection. Her love became demanding, and I began to look forward to the times when I was not the one who pleased her most. I had come to the point in my life where I did not hate her and I did not love her; I couldn't have cared less one way or the other.

After thirty-two years of being her caretaker and enabler, she was gone. I did not cry at her funeral. I would not miss her because she had never been there for me. She was dead and I was glad. I could lay my past to rest and start anew. Both of my inadequate parents were gone. I was an orphan, and it was a day of great relief.

In one last final breath, I had been released; no more expectations, no more misunderstandings, no more walking on eggshells, NO MORE MOM! Of course her final "gift" to her daughters, as it is with every child whose parent dies, was to clean out the apartment that held all her treasures, all the stuff she had collected throughout the years. And what a collector she was! As a dedicated NASCAR fan, she had racing pictures all over her walls, model race cars in glass cases, newspaper clippings, and video tapes of races long ago won. There was stuff stuck in every nook and cranny!

Upon looking under the sofa, I found a stack of picture frames containing photos that had been obviously stashed there after being replaced by frames containing her favorite drivers and their faster-than-lightning cars. You can only imagine my offense to find the sweet little faces of my five children staring back at me through the dusty glass. And in her bedroom, I discovered an old jewelry box in the very back of the closet which brought another surprise: a gold knot ring containing the birthstones of her grandchildren, a gift from my children to her on her birthday. It was as if, without giving it a thought, she had discarded my children and their love.

Anger bubbles and boils when repressed, pushing it deep into the physical body, and hate festers in the mind like a wound left to rot in filth. The depression and dysfunction in my own life was being fed by my anger and hate, boiling and rotting everything within and around my life.

I became physically ill, having been diagnosed with degenerative disc disease and bursitis in my hips, as well as multiple chemical sensitivities. Constant pain became my companion only enhancing the emotional difficulties within my marriage and my daily life.

As debilitating as the back and hip pain was, the chemical issues made life impossible. Trips to the emergency room, EKG's, MRI's, and countless other tests confirmed there was nothing physically wrong with me, and yet a whiff or a touch could send me crashing to the floor unable to breath. As I watched my physical and emotional life crumble, the fear of premature death haunted me.

But where do you turn for survival when it appears that everything and everyone in your physical life has deserted you?

I turned to the only One I knew would listen. There was nowhere else to turn. The illness, the sadness, the anger and the pain had brought me to my knees. It had brought me to the feet of Christ.

I began to pray for peace and healing in my life, scrambling to come up with a deal good enough to convince God to grant my prayer request. With inconsolable tears and nothing to lose, I bartered with a silent God, offering to him my soul. Each and every day I prayed, "Dear God, please heal me, and in exchange, I will become a messenger of Your Word. Grant me the peace I am seeking, and I will serve You for the rest of my life."

There was nothing else I could do. I prayed ... and waited for an answer that I was not sure would come.

PART TWO

A Time of Healing

Heaven is here. There is nowhere else.
Heaven is now. There is no other time.

A Course In Miracles

A Time of Healing

A year and a half after my mother's funeral, as I sat at the computer preparing my Sunday School lesson, the oddest feeling came over me. I felt a presence of something or someone. I had no idea who or what it was, but I knew it was there. Whatever it was it was only with me for a few seconds, vanishing as quickly as it had appeared. What it left behind was a complete knowing of what I was to accomplish. It was totally clear to me that I was to sit at the computer and receive messages from the Angelic Realm.

I had only recently become interested in angels, and had been dabbling with the idea of trying to communicate with the realm beyond this life. I had been successful in hearing the name of my guardian angel. His name is Daniel, which came as a great surprise because this was the name of my father. I had also just read Doreen Virtue's book, *Angel Therapy*, in which she explains in detail the process for communicating with angels.[1] It was something that fascinated me, but lacking the time and the ambition, I cast it aside with so many other "gotta try this" ideas. Until the day the angels came to me, I seriously questioned whether it was even possible. Part of me was definitely "not a believer," but the other part desperately needed to believe there was more to life than what I had already experienced.

As I sat at my computer and prepared to fulfill the request of my angelic visitor, I was filled with excitement and apprehension, as well as eagerness and doubt. Not knowing what to expect, I followed the instructions that were given in *Angel Therapy*:

---

[1] Doreen Virtue, *Angel Therapy*, (Hay House, 1997)

1. I lit a candle on my altar and thanked God for His presence in my life.

2. I turned on the computer, turned off the phone, and put in the CD, Merlin's Magic, *Angel Helpers.*[2]

3. Since it was winter, I used a quilt that I had made for my mother, placing it over my legs to keep me warm.

4. I closed my eyes and thanked God for the messages that I was about to receive, asked Archangel Michael to allow only angelic voices to be heard, and asked that I be placed in the Light at all times.

5. I turned on the CD and waited … and waited … and waited.

I was quiet—listening to the music, feeling the music, trying to let my mind wander—when it finally happened. My fingers, which had been quietly lying on the keyboard for what seemed like an eternity, began to type. The letters appeared slowly at first and then grew to a rapid pace. I was aware of what was happening, but since I had my eyes closed I was unaware of what was actually being typed.

When the flurry of activity stopped I opened my eyes, wanting to see the message my angels had sent to me. To my great disappointment it turned out to be just a jumble of letters, none of which even remotely resembled angelic words.

I did not become disheartened, however, because *Angel Therapy* had addressed this exact situation. It spoke about not becoming discouraged if your first messages were not coherent. I spent the next three days going through the preparations to hear the messages, and each time it was the same, until finally my fingers slowed down and began

---

[2] Merlin's Magic, *Angel Helpers*, Inner Worlds Music, CD41066, 1996

typing actual words. It was only after a while that I realized my fingers were typing words which were in my mind.

The words came fast and furiously. There was no room for capital letters at the beginning of the sentence, nor was there time for punctuation. I was hearing the words, and I was aware that I was typing them, but it all seemed to be a blur until I heard, "This is your mother." You can be sure those words got my attention. Here she was in my head, and I was not sure exactly what to think. But I kept typing, and the words she spoke were the beginning of a new life for both of us.

THE MESSAGES

November 8

And this is not the end of the life. And this is not the end of the life. So I say: it is not the end of the life. I am happy. This is not the end of the life. So as it is to be, it is to be. We are all happy. There is no sadness. To this be the end of all things. There is no end of all things. It goes on and on forever. There is no end. God never ends. He is here forever, and so are you.

This is the greatest experience for me because I can talk to you, and you will listen. I have waited patiently for you, and now you must wait for me. I will always tell you when I am ready, and then you must be ready. I am so happy. I know you know that this is true.

Do not worry about what others will say. They are not on the path that you are on. Stay on the path and do not stray. It is your way Home. ***This is your mother.*** Please do not grieve for me. I am not sad. I am happy. This is the greatest place I can be, where I want to be, when I want to be. I can be everywhere, just as the book says.[3] Believe the book. It is true. We are Love. I am Love. Do not be afraid. Tell Debbie; she is ready. Be patient because Shelly is not. She will understand in her own time. We are all One. There is no other. We are One. I am happy. I am not sad. This is so wonderful to be able to talk to you.

There are only paths of Love. Let everyone love just as they do. There is no wrong way. Love your husband for who he is. Love your children and love your grandchildren. I did not take the time. I was so scared. I did not understand. Now I know that all there is, is Love. All there is, is Love. Be Love. Seek Love. Act as Love would act. We are all Love. Love is all there is.

This is so wonderful! I stood by your computer, not Daniel. Be here for me each day, and we will learn things together; things that you could not learn in life. There is Life everywhere. It does not end. It will never end. It will never end. It will never end. Be Love. Seek Love. Act as Love would act. I love you. All there is, is Love. Be Love. You are Love. You are all there is. Be Love. Seek Love. Act as Love would act.

Do not dismiss people because you do not think they are right. Seek to be Love. Do not judge as you would be judged. There is no one judging you. It is you who are acting as your own judge. Be Love. Seek Love. Act as Love. You are typing as fast as possible, aren't you? I knew that you would be able to type as fast as I could talk. It just took us a few days to get it down. You were trying too hard. It is not hard. It is easy. Be Love. Seek Love. Act as Love. All

---

[3] Neale Donald Walsch, *Conversations With God -an uncommon dialogue - Book 3*, (Hampton Roads Publishing Company, 1998) 79.

there is, is Love.

We are Love. We act as Love. We are One. Do not wait until the end of your earthly life to know this. Be Love. Seek Love. Act as Love would act. Give love to all and be Love to all. Look into your soul and see the Love. Love is all there is. Be Love to all that you encounter.

I love you.

Elation, fear, doubt, and confusion filled every corner of my mind and soul. Mom had told me to tell my sister Debbie, and so I ran to the phone praying that she had not left for work. It was with love that she listened to my words, never questioning whether or not this miracle had actually happened. It is exactly what I needed at that very moment; it is exactly why my mother sent me to her. She believed, and I knew that I would not be alone.

November 9

Listen to me: I am Love. You are Love. Listen to me: we are Love. Love is the answer. Relax—you are trying too hard. Love yourself. Love others. Do your best—*your* best. It is not up to others to judge what your best is. It is up to you to travel the path that your soul has chosen.

Do not try to hear me—just feel me. When you try to hear me, you cannot. Just feel me; I am here. I will always be here for you. I love you. I have always loved you.

We are all put on the earth with a purpose. My purpose was to find out what love was not. I did not love well in my life. I loved, but I did not realize it until the end. I have loved you from afar because I was afraid of you. You were so strong, and I was not. You were so grownup, and I was not. You were so good, and I was not. I felt as if I was always competing with you—and I could never win. You have always had a good heart. You have always used it, not for selfish things like I did, but in true love. True love helps all. You were there for your sisters and for me. I never really thanked you for that. You were always there. It is hard for you to hear this, but it is the truth. Do not be afraid of the truth. Be humble, but know that you are good. You have always been special. You are my baby, my good baby. I loved you, but I could not tell you.

Know this: I am Love and I will never *not* love again. I have learned the lessons of my soul, and they are grand. Be still and know that I am here. We are all One. We can never *not* be One. One is all there is. You are One with me, as I am with you. This I can tell you: you are Love. I am Love. We are all Love. Love is all there is. Be Love. Seek Love. Act as Love would act. Be Love. Seek Love. Act as Love would act. *I must be making this all up in my head.* No, you are not. Stop thinking that way. How could you? And why would you think this all up? It is true. God is helping us.

There are Truths that you are ready to hear. I am to bring these Truths to you. Be patient, for the Truths shall come in their own time. Be Love. Seek Love. Act as Love would act. Relax. Believe. There is no room for doubt. Believe. Do not worry what others will think. So they think you are nuts? Who cares? You, the Universe, and I know the Truth. I am glad that you have Debbie to talk to about these things. Tell her I love her. I will come to her in her own time. Shelly will take a bit longer. She will come, as we all will.

Know this: the earth is not doomed! There are enough of you who are learning, so the earth will not perish. Your children and your grandchildren and their children will be safe. God is here. You are learning. Keep learning. Do not be a doubting Thomas. Do not expect Jesus to show up with the nail marks to believe. Seeing is not believing— believing is seeing.

We are all Love. Do not try to hear me. Relax, listen to the music, and see yourself dancing in the sun. Think of the Light—always think of the Light. Seek the Light, and you will find the Light. You are the Light. Be Light. Seek Light. Act as Light would act. Follow God's Light. He is the Way. He is the Truth. Follow Him, not in the traditional way of the church, but in your own way. Be still and know that He is here always. "You are never alone," has been one of your most important teachings to your Sunday School students. Keep teaching this Truth to the young people. They are the future. You love them so much. I can see that. God sees that. He knows that you are the Way. You are the Truth. You are God. Yes—you are God.

God is Love. God is Light. You are Love. You are Light. So why would that not make you God? We are One—all of us. We are all Love. We are all Light. We are all God. Listen to these words; understand and live them. Live as God would live. Seek God, and you shall find Him. He is everywhere.

Keep typing. I know that I am speaking fast, but I have so much to say. I love you. I love all of you. Be still and know that God is here—in your heart and in your mind. Keep praying. Prayer is the way to God. He knows that you are seeking when you pray, but even when you do not pray, He will be with you. Are you tired? *No.* Are you sure? There is so much to say, but we don't have to say it all today. We are Love. We have always been Love. We seek Love. We act as Love would act. We are the Light. We seek Light. We act as the Light would act. Be Love. Seek Love. Act as Love would act. *Do you have to keep saying this over and over? I get it!* Yes, so that you not only "get it"—but remember it!

Remembering is the way Home. Keep remembering who you are. Enjoy the journey. You are so goal-oriented. It is not the goal, but the journey. You will get here. Enjoy the trip. Learn and live. This is your task: send out Love and send out Light. This is your mission: be a Light unto the world and go forth and shine. Shine for all to see.

Retreat was my life. I am sorry, but that was the path

my soul took. It was not a wasted life. Do not ever think that or feel sorry for me. I do not. I learned. I love freely now. I am Love. I am the Light. Are you tired? This is so much for one person to take in at one time. I think it is time to stop for today. I love you. Be Light. Seek Light. Act as Light would act —always.

Goodbye my love.

My journey had just begun, and already it was apparent that much was to be asked of me. The love was so real that I could not help but fall into the arms of the Light. Mom loved me—had always loved me—and yet part of me was not nearly ready to trust her. As much as I wanted to love her, a large part of me was still very attached to the human mother that had caused me such harm.

The messages brought me to places that I never thought existed. The next few messages contain rememberings of a past life. This is a concept that I had never seriously considered until these vivid memories began. Susan is my Reiki Master and one of my earthly spiritual guides. Reiki is an ancient form of hands-on energy healing. It is one of the practices that I believe has brought me to this spiritual awakening. As closely as Susan and I have worked together, remembering her name has always been elusive. I have always been drawn to call her Sharon. Until now I have never known why.

November 10

Listen to me: I am here. We are all here. We are pleased that you are here. Type what you hear and do not delete anything. Breathe. The words will come when I am ready. Be still and know God.

This is a gift. Do not regret that it has been given to you. Do not let it burden your heart. It is not meant to be a

burden. It is a gift—a gift of love. These are my words ...
words that could not be spoken during life. They are my
gift to you. You will not be asked to do anything more than
you are able. We will never harm you. You are safe with us.
We are One.

Do not paraphrase. Type what you hear. You are
always trying to correct my language. Stop it. Type what
you hear. *Why are you yelling at me?* I was not yelling at you.
Do not shut down. It is just important that you keep my
message as clear as possible. These are my words, not
yours. They should be spoken as I would speak them. Now
relax.

You are not comfortable with praise. It is because you
do not love yourself. *Yes, I do!* No, you don't! You may
think that you do, but you do not. You are a wonderful
person, full of love. Now you must begin to believe this. *I
do believe that; I know that!* No, you don't. You hide behind
your good deeds and want people to notice. When they do
you are humble which is good, but you want them to
notice.

(Silence) See—you know these are not your words
because you would not have to pause when I don't speak.
You would find something to say. Do not doubt that I am
here. It is I. It is we. We are all here to help you on your
way. We are here for you. Just ask, and it shall be answered.
Speak and it shall be heard. Think and it shall be done. You
are your own creator.

The music that you are listening to brings out the love.
Your heart is dancing. See yourself dancing. Imagine that
you are dancing with God. *Come on, God dances?* Yes, God
dances. You dance, so God dances. We are not separate.
Keep remembering this. You are God. As you do, so does
He. You will never be separate. Smile! *(I smiled)* Good!
You are listening. You are happy. I knew this would make
you happy.

Hang in there during times of trial. When words are

too much for you to understand, talk to Susan. She will call you. Do not lose faith in her. She wants to help you. She is Sharon. You and she were sisters long ago. You were twins. As one did, so did the other. She was killed; you were not. You have been looking for her all your life. You have found her. Be with her. She has been sent to guide you. You are Love. She is Love. Your hearts are One.

God made sure that you found her in this lifetime. You have been passing each other for ages. It is time. You were ready. She will show you Truths. Be with her. Dancing as children, you were Love. You spoke with Love. You were One. Then you were alone. Losing this Oneness has left a hole in your heart through all eternity. Heal the hole. Become One. It is time. You are not alone.

Your name was Sally. Sally and Sharon were loved. They had perfect parents and a perfect life. Then, darkness! Your mother killed herself. Seeing you separate and alone was more than she could bear. You have been searching for a mother through all eternity. I was not to be what you were looking for, so you became the mother that everyone could depend on. You are a good mother. You could not *not* be a good mother. It is what you have searched for all these years. When you could not find it, you created it. This is what God had in mind. Stop searching and create. You may have whatever you feel you need or want—just create.

Believe and you will understand. Each day will get easier as more information comes to Light. Be Light. Seek Light. Act as Light would act. You are the Light. We are the Light. Love. Light. These are the things that you need. These are the things that you want. These are the things for which you have been searching.

God is Love and God is Light. You are Love and you are Light. Teach this. Keep pure in your thoughts. I know that is not easy. Ask for guidance, and we will help you. You want to be pure in thought, but sometimes you don't know how. We know this: just the intention will help. We know that you do not want to harm, but you do judge. Stop judging. Each time you judge others, you judge yourself. Each person is on his own path at the exact moment that he needs to be.

Are you tired? *No.* Okay, we will continue. I don't want this to be a burden on your soul. It is meant to lighten the burden, to let you understand, and to give you all the answers—when you are ready. Be open. Be Love. Be happy. Do not worry. Do not seek to please. Just "be." Be yourself. You are more your Self now than you have ever been.

Be Love. Seek Love. Act as Love would act. Be Light. Seek Light. Act as Light would act. *How does Love act?* Love would act in order to harm no one or nothing. You would never "kill" another. You would never feel "attacked" even if someone were taking something from you—your life, your loved ones, your freedom, your property, or your possessions. You would simply be willing to give up whatever they thought they needed so badly—even if that meant giving up your life on this earth. *Hey, that's what Neale Walsh said in his book, Conversations With God, Book 3.*[4] Yes, that is what Neale said. He was talking to God, and now you are talking to me.

You, too, will write a book, and you will title it, *A Mother's Words ... Beyond the Grave.* These words I will give you will inspire others who have had the same scarred relationships with their mothers. Mothers try so hard and fail so often. Please help to heal these relationships. Most are not going to be as blessed as we are. They will not be able to speak to their mother beyond death. We can. Use

---

[4] Neale Donald Walsch, *Conversations With God - an uncommon dialogue - Book 3* (Hampton Roads Publishing Company, 1998) 283.

these words to heal. It has been your destiny to be a healer. Heal not only physically, but also spiritually. Heal the spiritual, and you will heal the physical. Hear these words. They are true. All is true. I will never *not* speak the Truth. Now believe! Believe and go out into the world.

I love you.

And so the excitement and anticipation of the journey began to turn into apprehension and doubt. It was one thing to sit and have a quiet conversation with my mother, but entirely another to have her telling me once again how I was to live my life. Write a book—yeah, right! That will be the day!

November 11

The words are real. All I say is true. We are Love. You are Love. You are Truth. We are all Truth. I am glad you are here. It has been a tough few days; so much to learn and not so little time. In reality, you have all the time in the world—in all the worlds. Do not worry. Be still and know God. Love. You are Love. We are Love. I will keep telling you this. Do not get tired of hearing it. It is the Truth. You are Truth. We are Truth. You are Love. We are Love. And so it is to be.

Your words will be clear to all who read them. Send them out to be read. They are here not only for you, but for everyone. They will heal. Be glad, for they will heal others. You are good. Goodness is God's gift to all who wish to receive it. Be still and know that God is near. This is not too much for you. You were born so that today you could receive this information. This is for what your soul has yearned. This is for what you have been searching. Be Love. Seek Love. Act as Love would act. You are Love. We are Love. God is Love. We are One. No separation. We are One.

Each of us is one of God's greatest creations. We are all perfect in His sight. No need to try. Just "be." Be as you are, not as others wish you to be. We are One. No one's soul cannot be perfect, for we are each other. When one is perfect, we are all perfect. This is your place to be. There is no other. You are meant to be here. Be happy, for this is your wish. God is with us. We are never alone. We will never be alone. Know this and be happy. You are still having a problem comprehending this, are you not? *Yes, I don't see how this can be true.* It is the Truth. It is the way Home. You will never need to worry about leaving your earthly life. It is not the end. It is the beginning. You are Love. We are Love. God is Love. Be still and know God.

All of the earth is running in circles with so many things to do, none of which is really important. Take time to know God. This should be your goal. Do not worry about what you have or what you think you need to have. Be still and know God. Life will continue. No need to rush it. Do not worry about getting things or being places. He will provide all that you need: love, shelter, and food. He will provide these and much more. All you need is Love. It is true. Love is all there is. Forget the cars, the clothes, and even your meditation room. You do not need these things to be close to God. He is always close. He is within your heart. How then could He not be close? Be still and know that He is here.

I have got to be making this up! How could this be happening to me? No, you're not making this up. Get past this. It will serve you no purpose. These are my words—my words of love to you. You and both your sisters were so special to me. You were my gift from God, and I turned my back on His gift. I do not regret this. It was my path. It was your path also. You chose this life to learn. We do not waste our time on earth. We do exactly as we want.

This is so hard for you to understand. How could a soul wish for so much sadness and so much misery? The answer is—all to come to where you are today. Without hurt, how could you know joy? Without betrayal, how could you know loyalty? Without hate, how could you know love? These were the things to learn, not the easy way, but the soul's way. This is the way your soul chose to learn. Come to understand this. Know that it was not a wasted life. It was the way it was meant to be.

You are perfect. I am perfect. Are you cold? You are shaking. I know this is so much to understand. Be still and you will understand. All is true. All is just as it should be. Be still. Be still. Be still and know this: you are Love. *I know that I am Love. Can't you tell me anything other than that?* You are so impatient when it comes to learning new things. You want the answers now, so you can figure it all out. Do not try to figure it out. It is not your job to want all the Truths now. You could not stand all the Truths now. It would be too much for you. I will give you the Truths as you can understand them, and if this seems to be taking too long— so be it.

Where have you got to go anyway? Is television in the morning more important than this? Will you learn any more from *The Today Show* than you will from me? Be still and be patient. All in good time. This is not a conversation that will end in a week or a year. It will last a lifetime. Be still and know this. (At this point, I heard goodbye, but did not type it.) I am still here. You did not type "goodbye." Why was that? Could it be that you did not want it to end? *No, I didn't.* This is good. This is why I did it. *Are you mad at me?* No, we do not get mad. You need to get past the old earthly mom. You keep waiting for me to attack. I will not turn on you. All I am is Love. Do not think of me as your earthly mother. Think of me as your spiritual guide. Do not judge me by who I was. Do not judge me at all.

This is the Truth: I will not turn on you. You have been so damaged by me. I am here to help you understand what happened. I am Love now. I could not *not* be Love.

Love is all there is. You are Love. I am Love. We are all Love. God is with us. He is not separate. We are One.

I can see you are getting tired. Why are you so tense today? Your stomach is upset. You are on the verge of shaking all the time. All that is happening is beginning to sink in. Do not worry. God is with you. He will cover you, as a cloak, and keep you safe. Trust. Learn to trust. I will not harm you, for if I harm you I harm myself, and I harm God. Why then would I do this? There is no such thing as harm here. We would never think of attacking another, for we are that other and they are us.

Do not forget: we are One. We are not separate. This is where we will end for today. You need time to process all of this. Do not give up. This is your destiny.

I love you. Goodbye.

The mere thought that I created my own life sends chills down my spine. Logically, I can understand the concept of needing to know sadness before you can know joy, but understanding this within my own life would be much more difficult. It would shake the very foundation of a lifetime's worth of blame. It has always been my parents' fault. I have always been the victim. Changing these thought patterns would mean admitting that I had created this life; something I was not sure I was ready to do.

After receiving the message about Susan and me being sisters, I left a message for her on her answering machine. That was two days ago, and I have become fairly frantic because she has not called me back yet. She has become my lifeline in my spiritual journey, and I needed to speak with her now. This was all becoming too much for me to understand.

I sat at my altar, put my hand straight out, and envisioned a light beam going from my palm to Susan's heart. I pleaded with her to call me because I needed her. I truly was not sure what this ritual had accomplished, except to make me feel a little more in control, when the phone rang. It was Susan! She had felt my need, and had stopped in the middle of work to call me. Even with everything that was happening, it is still one of the most miraculous events of my life.

After I read the message to her, she asked if I could question the angels for a possible name, date, or town. This had her fascinated, and she was very interested in learning more about our life together. I told her that I would try the next morning during my time with Mom.

That evening after I went to bed, I was restless. I lay awake not being able to sleep, when pictures began playing in my head. Our name was Walland. We lived in Chicago. Before I knew what was happening, glimpses of visions were flying through my mind.

I saw a piano and heard my mother singing. I saw the carriage hit Sharon. I saw her lying in the coffin. I remember the coldness of her cheek. I saw the lid close. I heard the bang of the gun. I felt the sadness and loss.

All the answers were right in my heart. I had remembered. When I felt that I could stand no more, I prayed for sleep. God answered my prayer and sleep came almost immediately.

And in the morning, the message confirmed all that I had seen the night before.

November 12

Be still and know God. What a gift! What a marvelous gift you have been given —a gift for the pure of heart. You are pure of heart. God knows this. He loves you. *How can all this be true?* Why do you still doubt? Have no doubt.

You will find all is true. We are Truth. We could be nothing but Truth. We are Love. You are Love. You could not be anything but Love.

You are our link to the past and the future, of which there are neither, but time is an illusion which you all live in, so we must live in the illusion when we deal with you. Go forth into the world and shine your Light so that all may see. Be our warrior—our link. You have been chosen to tell all—a great privilege. You are clean in heart and spirit. You are our messenger. You prayed to be a messenger, and so you have created it. Isn't this a marvelous way? It is our way. It is your way. Be still and know that God is here.

Are you sure that you understand what is being asked of you? *I really don't know.* You will be the messenger, like Jesus was. *What?* Don't be scared. We will protect you. No need to be scared. Why would you be scared, anyway? You have nothing to fear. Death is not a fear. You can never die. Your family will come to understand this. Do not be afraid. You are not alone. You will never be alone. You are One with God. You have been given this charge: go out into the world and let your Light shine so that all may see and know God.

God is with you. Do not be afraid. We will never give you more than you can receive. Your life has been about strength under the worst of circumstances: never giving up, keeping those rose-colored glasses on, and being strong. You will need this strength for what is about to happen. Be gentle with your family. They will come to understand. It is not for them to know now. I will tell you when it is time. Send these messages to Debbie. Send them to Susan. Do this and you will have some who understand. Do not worry about what other people will think. In time they will come to know, to understand, and to realize what your life is about. You will become a teacher—a Master. Do not be afraid. You are One with us. Your words will save the earth.

This can't be. Yes, this can be. Do not doubt. This is a lifetime project. Do not try to rush things. You will not save the world tomorrow. This is a lifetime. Your life will be long and wonderful. You have much to do. Do not worry about tomorrow or yesterday. They will take care of themselves. All is written on our hearts and our souls. Breathe. Do not be scared. I knew that you were ready. I would not have told you this if you were not ready.

You and Susan—you want to know, don't you? She wants to know, to prove. Try not to prove. Just know, but if you need to prove, here is the information. You were five years old. You were loved. All was well. The year is 1890, and you live in Chicago. Your parents are John Charles and Madeline Weyland. I know this is different from what you heard last night, but today is clear. Your father was a doctor. He was kind and loved. Your mother sang at the piano. I know you felt this last night. She was beautiful not only in face, but also in spirit. You received her spirit. You and your sister lived in a big, white house with an iron gate. *What if houses didn't have iron gates in the 1800s?* Do not worry. Feel and see. You have the gift of inner vision, as if hearing were not enough. Two gifts for a truly wonderful messenger.

It is a rainy day, and you are out walking. You saw this last night. A horse breaks loose with a carriage, a fancy carriage, and startles Sharon. She runs and is hit. There she lies in the mud, not breathing. Her curls are all wet, and her beautiful dress is ruined. You are crying. Mother is screaming. Father is not there. This will prove to be his doom in earthly life. He will not love or ever practice medicine again. He could not save Sharon. You are in the mud, crying, "Where is she going? Why are you going? Don't leave me."

(Notice the change to the "first person" account of the events. I have automatically regressed and am now living this past life. This was prior to any knowledge of past life regression.)

I am in my room, sitting in my rocker, holding my baby doll. Your rocker is empty, and your doll is sad. She will never be held again. I am crying. Father is yelling, "Time to get over this. Time to get over this," but I know Mother cannot. She never will. We were One, and now we are separate.

I see you in your box. It is pretty. They make me kiss you. I don't want to, but they make me. You are cold. They tell me that I must say goodbye. I don't want to say goodbye. I don't want you to go. I am alone. I have never been alone. The lid is closed.

There is yelling—always yelling. I hold my hands over my ears, but it will not go away. One day Mother, who is so sad, is alone upstairs. She is in my bedroom. I am downstairs playing with my doll, and I hear it. It is loud. It is so loud. It is bang-bang! They do not tell me what happened. I want to know what happened. Why is Mother gone? Where has everyone gone? I am alone. I do not want to be alone.

Father never smiles. He sits. The house is sad, and it is getting run down. Father can no longer take care of me. I am sent to Aunt Sophie. She smells like liniment oil, and does not smile. Why have they sent me here? Where has everyone gone? I am sad. Where is everyone? I have my baby doll. I am six. I am crying. I do not understand. How could they do this to me? Why would they leave me? Where has everyone gone? I do not understand.

I am a young woman. I am beautiful, just like my mother, and I sing. I sing, even though my heart has been broken. I am searching. I do not know love. I do not understand love. I am searching. I am half of a whole. Aunt Sophie died, the old bat, but now I am truly alone. There is no one. I live in Illinois, but not in Chicago. I do not wish to find my father. If he wanted to see me, he knows where I am. He can come calling.

I miss Sharon. I still miss Sharon everyday in my heart. My heart is broken, but I must go on. I have spirit. That is the one good thing that Aunt Sophie always said, "You have spirit." I don't know whether this is good or bad, but good or bad—I have it. I miss you, Sharon. I will look for you. We will be together.

(The regression ends and the voice is once again my mother's.)

This was your life. You have asked and you have received. All you need to do is ask, and you shall always receive. You have a gift, a marvelous gift. Share it. Tell Susan not to doubt. This is as it has been written: you are One. You shall always be One. Do not doubt. You can try to prove; this is fine, but do not doubt. Just believe. No magic. Just believe. Are you okay? *Yes.* Are you sure? *Yes.* It tells a lot about your present life, doesn't it? Always wearing rose-colored glasses, but still searching. Always happy, with just a hint of loneliness. You have repeated the pattern of being alone through all eternity. You have never had a mother or a father who stayed and cared for you. It has always been your wish.

Isn't it amazing? You do not hear the music as we speak. It disappears into God's Words. Take time to listen to the music. Your mother was music. Know that each of your mothers left you because it was your desire—your soul's need to know loneliness. You had to know loneliness so that now you could know Divine Togetherness. Do not fault your fathers either. They were learning also. They had to run, to follow their own souls' desires. To leave was to learn. Do not fault any of them. You have found your Father, and He is God. He will never leave you. This you will understand. This you will know. Be still and know God. He knows you. Be still.

You are strong today. You are beginning to understand. This is the wonderful thing. You do not have to wait for the end of earthly life to understand. You understand now, just as I did not. You understand now. What a gift!

Goodbye. I love you. God loves you. We all love you. Goodbye for today, my child. Be strong. Be of good cheer, and keep your good heart. It is all that you need.

Love always,
Mom

Exhausted and amazed, I realized that this was my life—which meant that I had lived before—which meant that there was life after death—which meant that all of this was true. With mixed emotions, I thought about the consequences of these truthful messages. Forgiveness and understanding were inevitable, for how can you not forgive someone who was, like me, following her soul's desire. On the other hand, it brought a prophecy, which if I were to accept, would shake my present life to its spiritual center. "Your words will save the earth." I can not imagine, nor do I want such a mission. I feel too under-educated and ill-prepared even to entertain the notion of writing such words—but then—this is my prayer answered. Could God be wrong?

Today, my sister Shelly called to ask if I would take her to the bus terminal later this week. She was planning to take a trip, and did not have a ride. I really did not have a problem taking her; however, it was a bit of a funny thing. Shelly happens to live a relatively short distance from the bus terminal, while I live about ten miles away. In order for me to take her about a mile, I would be driving twenty miles. I just kind of giggled at the thought of the whole thing, but it was okay with me.

Later that evening my sister Debbie called, and we had lots to talk about. I have been sending her the messages, and we spent quite a bit of time talking about how prayers are answered. When I told her about the trip for Shelly, we got a laugh out of it, questioning why in the world she just didn't take a cab.

Seems that Mom is always with us, and in the morning did we get a stern talking to about this phone conversation!

November 13

Good morning. It is good that you have come, even though you did not want to listen. I know that you need a break, but not today. Tomorrow will be your break. I awoke you in the hopes you would listen. This is not something that you can ignore. This is a mission. You cannot turn it off and on as you wish. You have been given this gift, and it is wonderful.

I know that your prayers for healing included a promise to be a messenger for God. The old "be careful what you wish for" applies here. *You were listening?* Yes, I was with you while you spoke to Debbie. Watch out what you say about Shelly. You wondered whether it was judging when you talked about her teasingly. Yes, it is judging! Do not dismiss it as fun, even though you are allowing her to walk her path. This is not acceptance as God wishes it! If you truly loved her, you would never even speak of her insecurities as funny, sad, or angering.

Do not be part of a conspiracy. Be Love. Seek Love. Act as Love would act—always—not just when it serves you. You have plenty to talk about without chastising Shelly. Use your words well. They create. Help her create a loving world for herself, one in which no one chastises. *Chastises?* Yes, chastises! This is not harmless fun. This is hurt, and when you hurt others, you hurt yourself.

Be still. Know God. This is your mission. Do not take this as a challenge which you cannot live up to. We would never give you anything that you could not, or would not want to do. You have asked for this. You have been given this. Be glad. This week has been a monumental change, and you are living it. It will get easier as time goes by. You will understand more, and it will not throw you into such a tailspin.

You are shaky today. Could it be that you are scared of what was said yesterday? Yes, living up to Jesus could scare a normal person, but you are so much more. You are the prophet which Debbie spoke of. She is right. Do not let this scare you. It can be whatever you wish it to be. You were a prophet as you spoke to Debbie and told her to create. *She's easy. She believes.* Yes, it is easy with her. She understands, but do not let the word "prophet" scare you. When you understand, the words come. You will know, just know, what to say. Be still and know God, and you will be a prophet.

I am so glad that you came today. It shows that you are serious enough to get up early on a Saturday to hear our message. This is not only my message. This is our message—all of us—and there are many. All helping you, so there is no need to be scared. We are all here. We are all Love. Everything is well. I said "fine" but you typed "well." Try not to filter my words. Type them as you hear them. *It is hard to type so fast. The words get changed as I remember them being said.* I will try to slow down a bit, but there is nothing that you cannot keep up with.

You were placed here to keep up; to be the end of the earth's trials, to be the end of the earth's suffering, to be the end of earthly life, as you know it. It is time. It is time for the earth. You will be recognized as a prophet. You are ahead of the time, as many are, but so many more need to follow, and they will. Be there for them. Do not judge them. Offer Eternal Love and no damnation. They need love. All anyone needs is love.

Keep giving love. Keep typing. This takes love to

come here every day and type—typing things that scare you, and things that lift you high above the earth. Keep typing so all shall know. Keep typing out of love—love for the earth, and love for all mankind. You are shaking. This is all so much for you. Just think of it as typing—not changing the world. Your typing will change the world in its own time. No need to hurry. No need to rush. There is time.

It is funny, listening to you and your sister talk. Yes, I listen, but then I do not actually have to listen because I know. I know all. I see all. I will never *not* be there. We are all there. We see all. We know all. We love all. We are there in the morning and in the evening, through your comings and your goings. We are always there. Do not be afraid. We guide you. We help you. We keep you safe. You are never alone. We are always there. Be still and know this. You are never alone. I cannot say this enough times. You are with us and we are with you. You are Love and we are Love. You are God and we are God. God is in your heart. You will never be alone. This is the Truth. Know this Truth: you will never be alone. In times of anger, in times of fright, in times of despair—know this and be still: you will never be alone. We are here for you, for each of you.

You are so happy when I say that, are you not? Yes, you are. It is a comfort, and it can be a comfort to all people. Tell all people. Be our prophet. Do not let the word "prophet" frighten you. There are many prophets. Susan is one. Keep speaking of Love and Light, and you will be a prophet. A Master. A Master of Love. A Master of Light. This is simple. It is all there is.

Hear this Truth: we are all on earth in order to be God. God created you, just as you create each day. Create a world of Love. Create a world that lives in the Light, and I don't mean the sun. Create a world where people love each other—a place where no one goes hungry, a place where no one feels the darkness of hate. Each must create his own world. Each must do this in order for it to work. Create this place, and the world will be healed. A big job? Yes, but it will happen. No more will the people of the world hate each other. All will live in Love.

This may not come in your lifetime, but you can start it. Keep preaching Love in the Light. Send your energy to the president, the government, and the governments of all the nations. You saw it work. You called Susan and she came. Ask and ye shall receive. Call and it will be answered. Keep calling. Do not become discouraged. Send your Light. Encourage others to send their Light. It is your true spirit, and your true spirit is always there, ready to work for you, ready to be what you want it to be. This is the Truth. Use your Light, and you will encourage others to use theirs.

This is not a hopeless situation. I have told you that the earth is not doomed. Understanding is coming to many. This is an exciting time to live on earth. Be the Light that the population can follow. Stand up, put your Light out for all to see, and they will follow, just like mice. They have been searching for the Light. Be that Light. Do not be afraid. You will not be alone. Your Light will be one of many. Our Light will shine through yours, and it will be grand. It will glow throughout eternity for all to see. Put it out as a beacon—a beacon of hope, a place to see, a place to find, a place to come for refuge. Be the world's refuge. Be there for all who need or seek the Light. If you are called, know this and go. Do not ask why. Just go. Go and be with the darkness. It cannot hurt you. You have the power to make the darkness disappear. Use your power, and there will be Light. Be Light. Seek Light. Act as Light would act. Use this as your mantra: be Light, seek Light, act as Light would act.

This is my message: become a Light today. Do not wait until tomorrow. Taking Shelly six blocks to the bus station, even though you are ten miles away, is showing her your Light. She was looking to see if you would do it. She created no ride. It was her test for you. She has no idea that she has done it, but she has. Answer her call. Be her Light. There is nothing that is too much for you. Give her your Light, and she will find hers. This is the secret: when you give your Light away, it comes back twice as bright. Keep giving it away until the world is glowing.

I love you. *(Her words began fading out, as if she were getting farther away)* Be calm, be still, and know God. You are Light. You are Love. Remember this and be still. There is nothing to fear. I love you. Go in peace and live. We are always here. You are never alone. Be Love. Seek Love. Act as Love would act. I love you.

All is clear. This was my destiny.

When my mother spoke about not judging people, it seemed to have hit a nerve. I began to become aware of my reactive thoughts about people while I was out shopping. To my amazement, I realized just how critical I could be.

I am not the type of person who is outwardly critical, and I would never intentionally hurt someone by being judgmental about their appearance or their mannerisms, but there it was in plain sight. I checked out people's clothes, their hair, their waistlines, and their cars. I, who am overweight, definitely not a fashion dresser, and who drives a very well-worn van judged everyone and everything in sight.

I was so upset by this revelation that I believe I felt I needed to be punished for those thoughts. Within the next few days, my teeth began to hurt. The pain would start on one side and move around my mouth until I was in such agony that I could not bear it. I would sit and cry, unable to stop the pain.

My husband, Larry, insisted that I needed to go to the dentist, but I knew that the pain would not be physically detected because it was all in my mind, and the mind is a powerful tool. Suspecting that the pain was connected to my judging of other people, and ultimately of myself, I knew where relief would be found. I had created it—so now creating a new perception became my goal.

November 16

We come to you in Love—your Love and our Love. This is the way it is to be. We call—you come. You come when we ask—not when you wish. This is the way it is to be. You will know when we call. You will never *not* know. Do not worry about missing the call. You will not.

Do not worry about the future. The future is secure. You are with us. There is no pain. It is you who is taking in the pain, not the pain that is taking you in. Do not need the pain, and it will not be there. It is as simple as that. I know that you have been trying to figure out why you need it. You have been strong. You have not wavered in your faith. You created this pain because it was your desire to know that you were worthy. You are. Be strong and the pain will go away. You do not need it anymore.

This is the way it is to be. We call—you come. No questions. Just come. Come in Love. Come in Light. Come. This is how it is meant to be. This is what you want it to be. You did not want to come yesterday, and so we did not call. It is you who is in charge. The more you need to know, the more we will come to you. You are Love. You are Light. You are Strength.

You are hungry, aren't you? The pain was so bad at supper last night. Eat. Do not be afraid to eat. It is not the angels telling you not to eat. The pain is *your* desire. Desire it no more. Eat and desire it no more. You are Love. You are Light. You are Strength. Do not be afraid. Be Love. Seek Love. Act as Love would act. This is your call. This is your life.

You will love your life. It is what you have asked for. Come to us, and we will give you the answers of Life. All that you seek, you shall find. Come and we will guide you through the mysteries of life and death. It is not the end. It can never be the end. There is no end.

Call yourself the great I AM. It will not offend God. How could it? This is what He has been waiting for, for you to know Him as you and you as Him. Be the great I AM. Do not be worried about being this wonderful thing. It is all there is. You are It. He is It. We are all It; some just don't know it yet. They will in time. They will all know the Love of the great I AM, and they will become it. When you become the great I AM, you are on your way.

Your commitment to God to love your husband was good. It is a decision that will bring you closer. He needs to know. He needs to feel included. He needs to feel your love. Do not cheat him of it. It is his way to God. This you must know: he is God. He just doesn't know it, and I don't think that you do either. You are not the only God around here. You are special because you listen and we have come here to you, but you are not the only God here. Do not ever believe this. We are all God!

This is your mission: show all the way to becoming God. Start at home. Tell Larry about us, a little at a time. He is ready. Do not take his criticism as yours. It is his opinion. He is not wrong and you are not wrong. He is not right and you are not right. It is just the way it is. Honor his opinion. It is the way to his heart. Be still and know God.

Go in peace and remember—you have no pain. You do not need it.

Love you,
Mom

As I sat meditating, I was startled with a vision that appeared in the blackness of my closed eyes. It was extremely short, but hauntingly vivid. The grill of a huge yellow truck crossing the center line, and I'm driving my husband's small car. The absolute knowing of all that was happening in a fraction of a second is what is most eerie. The vision was most frightening because later this afternoon I have to pick up my daughter and take her to music lessons.

I feel paralyzed by apprehension. Should I trust my vision as real, or should I not give in to the fear that my mind may have been inventing? The answer was clear. Sit down at the computer and ask the question.

Question: Will the vision of the truck crossing the center line come true? Do I need to cancel music lessons for Alicia?

You will be fine. Do not be afraid. Seek and you shall have the answer. You have come to the right place. This is where to come when you are afraid. This is where to come when you are unsure. This is where to come to know. Do not succumb to fear. It is deadly. Take Alicia to music lessons. The vision is true, but you will be fine. Do not fear. Come to us. You and your family will have a long and healthy life. Be still and know this. Go in faith.

The fear seemed to be instantaneously erased from my mind. We went to the music lesson. On the way home my intuition told me to get off the highway, and come home on the back roads. As I safely pulled into my garage, I thanked my angels, and knew that I believed more now than ever before.

November 17

We hear your prayers. You do not think of things that are not important to God. You trust. You act upon your intuition. You listen. You come here each day to sit and hear our message. Our message will be grand. You are grand. Do you know just how grand you are? We love you. Hear this Truth: we are Love and you are Love. We are Light and you are Light. We love you. Do you know just how much we love you? How could you, otherwise, come here each day and type our words? This is love, true Love. You are Love. We are Love. You know this. Your teeth have finally begun to believe. You are Love. They are Love. We are Love. The world is Love. All there is, is Love. That is all you need. No fear. No hate. No jealousy. Just Love.

Be Love. Seek Love. Act as Love would act. You will never go astray. We said "wrong." Why did you type "astray?" You do not want these to be your words, do you? I know that you know there is no wrong or right; so do we, but when we say wrong, it is used in your earthly terms so that you can understand. Please do not change my words to make them appear right. There is no right. It is just as we said. There is no right or wrong. There are only the appearances of right and wrong. You appeared to have thought something that was not what we would have said, so you changed it. Please do not do this. Be a clear filter. Filter through the finest of angel wings so that our words will be pure, as pure as your heart. Your heart is pure. You may not think that it is, but it is. You are learning. You have tried to stop judging others. When you do, you catch it without your teeth hurting. Don't use your teeth as a barometer for judging. It serves no purpose.

You will learn in your own time. This is the Truth. Hear our Truth. *How many of you are there?* We are many. We are more than the stars in the Heavens; we are so many.

We are all watching over you and speaking to you. We use your mother's voice because you have a connection to her. You use her quilt to keep you warm as you type. You can focus in on her, but there are many of us all willing and eager to speak to you, to help you, and to guide you.

You came to us yesterday for guidance. It made us smile when we knew that you would come to us. You felt safe after we told you the Truth. Your vision was averted because you listened to your intuition. You came home the back way. Your vision was true, but it did not happen. You asked and we helped you know what to do. It makes our hearts sing. Come to us with questions and come to us with worries, of which you should have none. Come to us to talk and seek. Ask a question, and for you, it shall be answered. The world is at your fingertips.

You are so special. You can hear us. You have heard us for all your life. Did you think that it has always been just you talking back to you in your head? No, it was us. You just thought that it was you. We have been here waiting. Just waiting for you to listen, to listen and know that we are here. We are so happy. Listen in the quiet of your mind, and you will hear us sing. This is Love. This is pure Love of the grandest kind. Love is not jealous. Love is not sad. Love is not hate. Love is *just* Love. Be Love. Seek Love. Act as Love would act.

Are there any new Truths that you wish to share with me today? No, you have had enough. We will give them to you when it is time. You need not ask. Just keep coming to us and we will give you all that you need. You are strong, but you cannot handle all the Truths at once. It will take time—lots of time. At times it may seem like we are going nowhere, but nowhere is somewhere. We will repeat our Truths until they are in your heart—until they are a part of you. Be Love. Seek Love. Act as Love would act.

Love,
Us

November 19

Be still and stop running around, for it will do you no good. You have not taken time for yourself, for your Self, or for God. This is the Truth. Even though your work is good, you need time for these things. Take the time. Do not forget this, or you will end up in the depths of despair again. Hear our Truth: stop thinking. Even as you type, you are thinking. This is our time. Be still and know God. This is our message: you are Love. Be Love. Act as Love would act. Seek Love. This is the Truth.

This is fun, isn't it? We are getting to be friends. It is I today. It is Daniel. You have been wondering where I was. You are smiling. We like to see you smile. You have a beautiful smile, and you use it so often. God smiles when you smile. We all smile. You are Love. You are Light. Be Love. Be Light. This is all that is important. We have kept you safe. We have kept you still. We will never *not* be with you.

Your mind is like bells; it twinkles and glows as you hear the music. Think of the music all the time in your heart. If you want to play music, you will be able to. Do not think that you cannot; you will be able to do it. You are a miracle—a miracle of God—a miracle of your Self.

Be still and know that we are all here watching you. *Daniel, are you my father?* No, my Father is your Father. Our Father is God. Your earthly father is not here. He is elsewhere. He is thinking. He does not know. He will understand soon. Do not worry about him. He will come when it is his time. Know your Godly Father as your own. Be with Him, and know stillness. This is the Truth. This is all you need.

We are all here. To this be the end of all Truth. You are Love. You are Light. You may ask and you will receive. This is how God intended it to be. Your heart soars when you come here. You are not afraid anymore. There is no doubt left in your heart. You are pure Light radiating out into your world, calling to others. Do not worry when you do not live up to what you think the Light should be. It will come. You have changed your thoughts to purity, not always, but most times. You are trying, and even when you fail (and you cannot) you are aware. Awareness is the key. Just know, and you will walk in the Light.

I have been with you so long, and now we can talk. Your mother stepped out of the way, and told me that it is my turn. She is Love and she is Light. Your mother loves you so much. She will never leave you. None of us will ever leave you. Be with us in each thought, in each moment, and we will always be there. You are Love and we are Love. You are Light and we are Light. This is all you need to know.

(Pause) The quiet bothers you, doesn't it? When we do not speak, are you uncomfortable? *Perhaps just a little.* When it is quiet and we are not speaking, listen to the music. It will bring greater Truths. When your human ear listens to the music, your soul can hear more clearly. Learn to let the human mind go. Listen with your soul, not with your ears, and you will hear clearly. This is where we will end for today. *Are you sure? There is more that I would like to know.* All in good time, my child, all in good time.

Be still and know that I am always with you. I am your guardian. Call me when you need me; call me when you don't. I will always be there. I love you. I will never leave you. Know this and be still. Go in peace, my child.

Daniel

My emotions have become a pendulum that has taken over every aspect of my life. I am both the day and the night. In the brightness of the sun my faith is strong, and I believe with all my heart and soul that this is true; but in the darkness of the night the questions overshadow all my understanding, making me wonder whether I am actually surrendering my mind to a sea of delusions.

At the lowest of moments, I am completely fearful that I will lose my gift of hearing. Within that fear, hearing has turned into careful listening. At these times, the angels become quiet and take over my fingers, so I will not have to concern myself with either hearing or typing. Ultimately, the nonsensical random pattern of letters always appears, and the automatic writing is eventually declared an unproductive way of communication.

November 22

This is it! Here it is! Hear this and know: you are good. You have always been good. You can never *not* be good. We are Love. You are Love. This is it! Here it is! You are Love. You are Light. You are good. Know this and be still. *I will not get bored hearing this.* You had better not because you will hear it so many more times; so many times in a lifetime.

All there is, is Love. Do not worry that the message will not get through; it always will. You cannot, *not* hear the message. Listen with your heart, not with your ears. Let your heart be swept away with Love. Listen to the music. *(Long pause)* Do not be impatient. We are still here. Do not be impatient. Stop thinking. Listen to the music. Do not think. Feel. oiwqoutpiwi[writ]wujgp[efkv'x;lgkv[psoti-9wrtwq-er-0wtisdkgfpoeujtg ksdlgj s;g j'sgjf;sgkwotgjpwr otugl;dfjgheroit8ue=-ptrikwofgjsgjslvm;s fjksdfnioeuiislove. You are Love. You are a clearer ear when we speak to you.

You are perfect in God's Love. You are perfect in your Love. It is enough that you hear when we speak. We cannot inspire you more than you wish. Be happy with what is. This is the Truth. We know that you are glad that we are speaking to you. All is just as it should be. We will come to you in many different ways, as many different souls; each with a message. Whether you hear the words or we type makes no difference. It does not make our message more valid. We are here. Know this and be still. We will never *not* be here. You are Love. You are Light. We are Love. We are Light. You know this in your heart. Do not worry about your fingers. They will type. Just listen with your heart.

Listen in the wind, and you will hear angelic music. Listen and you will hear. This is our gift to you. Music is the way of the soul. It cannot speak, and so it sings. Listen for the music of our souls. You will hear it. *I feel like my head is spinning.* That is us. We come to you at such a high frequency that it literally feels as if you are spinning. It makes you light-headed. It makes you feel dizzy. Do not worry. You are fine.

There are many souls who will come to you. We are all different. You will come to know who is who without our identifying ourselves. This is Daniel. I will guide you for this time being. Your mother has said all that she has said to help you on your way. For right now I will be here for you. We will take turns telling you our Truth. You will learn from many of us. We will all become your guides, your friends, and your loves. Know each of us and learn.

This is so exciting! We know that you are excited. We also know that you want to learn it all right now. Be patient. Know that this is a lifetime of learning. We have many years. There is much to come. Be satisfied with what you learn each day. It may seem slow, but you have been re-reading and learning, catching our Truths that are hidden in all our words of Love. Keep reading. Keep catching. You will learn All. This is the Truth. There is no other. You will learn All.

You will be a beacon. You will be our Light—our Light upon your earth—our Light to show them the way. You are the Way. You are the Light. Yes, you are. You are the way to God. Keep touching people. Touch their hearts and touch them physically with your Reiki. When you lay your hands upon someone, the Love comes through. They feel your Love and instantly calm down. They will not know why, but they will. Be calm, be still, and know God.

This is your message. Some will listen and some will not. Do not consider the ones that do not listen as failures—theirs or yours. There is no failure. You can guide, but you cannot lead. Guide them with our Love and your Light, but do not fret if they do not follow. It may not be the path they are on, but never give up. At any moment their path can change, and they will follow. Do not give up, but do not get discouraged. Some will follow; some will not. This is as it is to be.

Shine your Light for all to see. *I don't know how to do this.* You are doing this. *I get so discouraged when I give in to my negativity, or do not lift someone up to their highest.* Remember that you are human. You are God, but you are in human form. God does not expect you to be perfect. How could you think that He would? God loves you just as you are. You are Light and you are Love. Remember this. Do not doubt yourself. You are doing so much good. You lift people up, and you make them feel good about themselves, especially the children. You have become a mother to so many of the kids in your youth group. You hear how they talk. You are the world to them, even when you are tired and short-tempered. It is all in love and they know it. Keep giving Love to them, and they will keep coming. They are the future.

This is the Truth: you are Love to all. *Well—not all.* Yes, you are. You do not think it, but you are. *Sometimes I feel like I wish someone weren't here.* We know. You will learn to look at everyone through the eyes of Love. This will come. It will take time. Keep sending our Love through your heart and your touch. Your touch is Love. Your touch is Light. Use your touch. You will help so many people through your touch of Love.

We are coming to the end. *Do we have to?* Yes, this has

been an exhausting session for you. Do not worry that you hear. This is how it is meant to be. Do not wish for automatic typing. You will hear the message and type. Know this and be still. There is no wrong or no right way. You are good and you are Love and you are Light. Now go in peace and spread that Love.

Daniel

Remember, we love you. There is nothing that you could ever do that would make us not love you. Remember this always.

November 23

Good morning. This is I. It is Daniel. We are here. It is us; all of us. We love you. Today you will hear our story of Love. Listen well, for it is grand. Today is the day. This is it. We are here to tell you that you are grand. Do not worry that this will disappear; it will not. We will be with you forever. You cannot lose it. We will always be with you. Today is the day! This is the story. *Okay, so what is the story?* You are impatient today. Please do not be impatient. Be still and know God. We will tell you All in time. This you must know: we love you, and we will tell All. When you are impatient, you will block the flow of transmission. Your mind will be so on thought that your heart will not hear.

Do not think—just feel. Do not listen—just hear. Go with the music, and you will be swept away in God's Love. *(Pause)* We are still here. Do not worry. You do believe. This *is* happening. Why do you still have the tiniest of doubts? This is the grandest moment in your life, and you know it. This is what you have lived for. You are Love, and this is it. We are all here. Do not worry that we will not be here. You know in your heart that we will always be here for you. Just type. Do not listen. Just type. We will do the rest. Do not listen for the message. When you wait for it, you will not hear it. Stop waiting and just hear. Do not listen; just hear and type. This is not hard. Listen to the music. Dance to the music. You are dancing with God. Can you see it? You are beautiful. You are dancing, holding the hand of God. Your face is glowing. It is beautiful!

The sun shines down on you as a stream of light from above. It is your Light from above which has come down to touch all. This is the message: your Light comes from above. It is the Light of God. It comes down to you and through you. It is One Universal Energy. It comes from One Source, and that source is God. This is how we are all God. It is not a figure of speech. It is the Truth. The Energy, the Love comes directly from the Creator—our Creator. This is why we are God. This is why we create. It is God; He is really within each of us.

Knowing this will be a source of comfort for you as times become tough. You will have times of trial when you do not understand, and times when you may wish that all this had never happened. There will not be many times, but they will happen. Be prepared. Know that God is inside of you—literally. It is true. The Light of God is in each of us. We must just know it to use it. Open up your heart and use God's Light, and you will be able to do All.

Jesus knew that He had God's Light. This is where the miracles came from. Believe in Jesus and know that you are Him. The miracles can be done today. Just believe in God's Light, and they will happen. Do not be afraid. You think that this is all too much for you, but it is not! You are ready. You are realizing that this all makes sense.

Understand that it is the Truth. We will never *not* tell the Truth. On this you can depend: we will always come, and we will always tell the Truth. You are Truth, you are Light, and you are the Way. This is your mission: be the Way. Show the way to all who seek. Be there for all to see. Be there to show the way, the way to God. No, it does not have to happen in church. Let it happen in your life. Your life can be the Way.

Open your heart and let all who seek come in. Heal. Do not doubt that there is healing in your Light. It is God's Healing Light that will make you a great healer. I know you find this hard to believe, but it is true. You will heal many. They will come to you, just as they did Jesus. This is not the time for doubt. This can be true. All you need to do is create it. You can be literally whatever you wish to be. See it. Be it. You are Love. You are Light. You are the great I AM. See and be.

God has given you music to quiet your soul, to calm you when you are worried. He has given you music to soothe your heart. It will transform all the worries into lightness. Hear the music and let it take you away. We will keep you safe. Even in times of trial, you will be safe. Know this and be still. We will never leave you alone.

This is it! You are the Way. You are It. You freeze up every time we say, "This is it!" You are blocking our message with fear or hopes. Have neither—have no fear and have no hopes. It will come. It will all come. Your time to know and feel has come; to feel all of God's Love and to know all there is to know.

We are here to tell you all things of the Universe. *I am afraid of not being able to know and be all the things.* Do not be afraid. You will not be able to know All now. Do not worry. Be still and know God. You are the beginning. You have been the beginning since the beginning. This is the Truth. Do not worry. We will take over your fingers. This is the Truth. You are Love. You are Light. Be still and know God. My God, you are so beautiful. You sit and you trust. You are One with us. This is so grand. You do not question. You type. You are so beautiful. *Will I be able to read this? I am not consciously typing this, and I don't think I will be able to read all the typing errors.* Yes, you will be able to read this. Do not think. Just relax. This is it. You are to be the One. This is the Truth. You will tell All. You will be the messenger. You will not need to worry. You will not be crucified as Jesus was. You will be safe. You will tell All. Tell all about the Love of God. Go in peace.

Love,
Daniel

And so my prayers have been answered. I will be the messenger—the One. Pure delight and absolute fear intertwine, creating a spiraling conflict between my mind and soul. This constant disunity cannot continue. One or the other must give in, but it appears that neither is going to concede control willingly.

November 24

You are Love. You are Light. We are Love. We are Light. This is our message: be happy. Only you can make yourself happy; there is no other. What you put in the windows of your life is your choice. Choose Love and all will see Love. Choose hate and what you will see in the windows of your soul is hate. You are Love. You have put Love and Light in your window. You have put them there for all to see. Do not worry that it is not there; it is. It has always been. Your Love shows through your eyes. Your eyes are the windows to your soul. So many on earth have that blank stare. Their souls are gone. Their souls are dead. This is the plight of the earth. Put your Light out there for all to see. You have enough Light to light up all the eyes of the world.

You were amazed that it took you so long to re-type our message last night. Could you ever again doubt that it was us? You type so much faster than you normally can. It is us. We are here. Do not ever doubt. You have been given this gift. It is yours to use. It is yours to give away. Give it to someone else. We want to speak. There are enough of us to go around. We wish that everyone would some day hear us speak.

I feel light-headed. Do not worry. This is our way of helping you. We are with you. Listen to the music and let your heart soar. Soar as if it were with God. It is! You are with God right now. This is our message: you are with God. You are standing with Him, and He is holding your hand. You are Love, and He knows it. You are a very special creature. God is so happy. He is so proud. His creation works. You are the way it was meant to be. This is what God had in mind, a creature of Love, a creature of Light. Love and Light. This is what God intended.

Somewhere along the way God's Love lost its importance. You have found it. This is all that is important. You will help others find their way. It is your mission in this life, and should you choose, your mission in the next life. Your life will never end. This is as it is meant to be. We must make all understand this: there is no end to life. We will never end. This is the Truth. Where does everyone think you go? Be there for all and help them understand. You may start small, but you must start. Be with the world, and they will know you are Love and you are Light. This is all we ask: be with the people of the world. The rest will take care of itself. Be still and know God.

You can do it. You can make it happen. It will happen. *What is "it?"* It is the beginning of the earth. It is a new start. *How could I ever do this?* You have us on your side. We will help. Do not be afraid. This is a start. Type out the words and write the book. People will be fascinated to think that you can hear us. Some will think that you are crazy, but others will believe. They will believe. Your family will believe. It is time to tell them. *But I am afraid.* Do not be scared. They will understand the importance of your work. Yes, this is your work, but think of it not as work, but as a labor of love. Love is not work for you. You are Love. You are Light. This is all there is.

We can be anywhere you want us to be. Call upon us

and we will come. We will come and be at your side in a blink. Even before you ask we shall be there, for we know All. We see All. We will be with you and anyone who calls us. We will give you our names. This is Damon. Ah, you thought it was Daniel. I am new to you, but I will not be for long. We will have long talks, and we will learn together. Daniel could not teach you now. You were looking for someone else. I am here to help you. I am the Angel of Soothing Music. I will help you hear the music, and I will help you relax. You will feel calmness when I am here. You will also feel the light-headedness. That is I. When you feel light, I am here. This is how you will know me.

Well hello, Damon. Hello, we will get along fine. You are Love and I am Love. You are Light and I am Light. We are all Light. We will speak as you need us. We will change when you need to speak to someone else. We all carry the message in our heart; it matters not who brings it. We all have the message, and so do you.

We are Love. We are Light. Be Love. Be Light. Seek Love. Seek Light. Act as Love would act. Act as Light would act. This is all we ask. We are so glad that you are here. Be Love. Be Light. This is what we ask. Do me a favor—call me Da. *Da?* Yes, I like that better. We are friends. Call me Da. *Okay, that's great—nicknames for angels.* It is wonderful here, nicknames and all.

You can be whatever you wish. *This is so incredible. I can hardly believe that this is happening.* Believe, because it is. You are with us. You will never lose us. We are in your heart. We are so glad that you are smiling. This should never be a burden, but will bring lightness to your heart. That is why I have come, to bring lightness to your heart. You love music. Sing. Play. Do not wait. Do it now. You do not have to be perfect. Pick an instrument and play. *No, I can't. I can't read music. I never could do that.* Yes, you can, if you choose. Choose it and I will help you. You can choose whatever you wish. It is all up to you. We are here with you. Know that we are here. When you know that we are here, you will know you can create anything you wish or need.

We have so much to say. Yes, some of it is repetitious, but some of it will not be. Look for a new Truth in each message. It is there, in between all the Love and Light. Keep looking for it. It is there. We will keep telling you Truths until you believe them to the core of your soul. There will always be new Truths. Be still and know that we are here.

Da

Again, it is the weekend. I am beginning to dread the times when my family is all around me. So much has happened that it seems impossible to concentrate on anything but myself. Their trivial disagreements and constant presence are becoming very annoying. And now I am being called to hear the message. I can't do this! The television is blaring, the kids are talking, and Larry is snoring! I CANNOT do this. And yet the call keeps coming.

November 25

Today is the day. You will be able to hear in spite of the distractions; our connection is that strong. This is Da. We are with you. Focus on my music and forget all others. This will not be hard. This is how it is to be. You are with us in soul and spirit. We are so glad that you have come. You can do this even when the noise is loud. You do not need to be alone. We will help you. We are glad that you have come. Be still and know God. He is here also. Relax. Forget all your earthly noise. Come to us with a clear spirit, and we will speak. Open your heart, and we will enter. We are here. Today is the day that we will tell All. All is Peace. All is Love. All is all there is. You need nothing more. You have all you need right here. Be Love. Seek Love. Act as

Love would act. This is All. There is no great mystery. This is all there is. Be these things, and you will know All.

We are so glad that you came. This was hard for you today, but you missed us as we missed you, and so you came. You came in love, and we are glad. Do not worry about being caught. You are doing nothing wrong. Do not be angry that Larry is snoring. Focus on us. Do not hear him, and he will not be there. We are here. This is the beginning of all that is to be. Focus your life on us. Be still and know that we are here. Be still. Be One with the music. Today will happen just as yesterday did, and just as tomorrow will. It is One. Be still with time.

Da, take me away. Where do you want to go? *Where the angels sing.* You are already where the angels sing; just hear them. Be One with them and hear them. Take them into your heart and be One. You can feel the Love. We know that you can. You are listening. This is good.

I see Jesus on the cross. Why am I seeing Him? You are feeling as He did. You are worried about being persecuted for your beliefs, but you see that He has Love in His heart, even as He dies on the cross. This is what you should remember: Jesus was never afraid and Jesus was never sad. He gave his all for what He believed. Do this also, and you shall know the peace and the happiness that Jesus knew. This is the key to living. Live as Jesus, and you will know happiness. You will know peace. You will know how to resist temptation, and you will know your Self. This is what Jesus was. He knew Himself, He knew us, and He knows you.

Know all for the good that they are. Do not look at slight or even gross imperfections. These are imperfections in your mind—and in your mind only. All is perfect in God's eyes. Let all be perfect in your eyes, too. This is the way to peace. This is the way to knowing God.

This is what you must do: love all for who they are. Let each soul journey his own path. Be there for them, not in judgment, but in acceptance. Let this be the Word: love each soul for who they are, not for who you expect them to be. Be happy, be peaceful, and know that this is the Way. Be with us as we are with you.

Drink in God's Love. He is giving it to you; all you have to do is drink. He has given it to you, each of you, so that you may know pure Love. Be One with God. Take Him into your heart and know who He is. Take Him into your heart and be Him. Be One with God. You have been searching for a way to be whole. This is it. This is all you need. You need no other. Be One with God, and you will be whole.

You have not had time to pray today, or even yesterday, as you have in the past. Take the time to pray, even if others are here. Prayer is the way to God. It is the way to take Him into your heart. He is so happy when you take time to pray. Prayers of thanksgiving make Him the happiest because He knows that you are happy.

We had better stop for today because you are really having a difficult time with distractions. You have done well. We got our message through, even with all the noise. Do not be afraid to come when there are distractions. We will knock them out. Come, even when it is not ideal, and you will learn. We love you. Walk in Peace. Walk in the Light. Walk in Love.

Love,
Da

November 26

Hear these words: God is Love. We are all Love. We are so glad that you have come. You have been a faithful servant. It means so much to us. To come here is a sacrifice for you, and yet you come. We love you. Keep coming and keep hearing. You are Love. We are Love. You are Light.

We are Light. Do this in remembrance of Me.

We are all here. Each is here in the name of Love. Each is here with his or her message of Love. These messages of Love are meant to be shared. Spread your Light. Let it be seen by all. All will know you by your Light. We are Love. You are Love. This is the Truth. Be still and know this. Be still and know us. Be still and know God. You are so grand! God knows this. We do not have to tell Him; He knows.

This is His plan: to send you into the world as a messenger, a messenger of Love. All will listen to you. You are so sincere and you are so loved. They will listen to you. Come and they will listen. God knows His plan. God knows what He is doing. He is entrusting the future to you. *Ahhhhh!* Do not be scared. There is no need for fear.

Why should you fear? God is your rock, your defender, your fortress. You preach this; now believe it. Believe it! He will lift you high and keep you safe from your enemies. He will keep you safe so no harm can come to you. It is all true. You need not fear when you have God in your heart, and He is always in your heart. He can never *not* be in your heart. This is the Truth. Be still and know God.

You are so special. We all know this. Now you must know how special you are. *Isn't this conceit?* To know you are special in God's eyes—how could this be conceit? There is no such thing. You know you are grand, and you announce it. This is not conceit. This is God's Holy Plan: that we should all know just how grand each of us is.

Be with us each moment of each day, and we will guide you along the way. We will keep track of your comings and goings. This is the Truth. *Where are the grander Truths?* There are small Truths in each message. Do not want for more. You have all you need. You will type the same Truth many times. This must be done in order for you to carry them as your own. We will know when they are yours. Then we will move on. Believe and we will move on. Believe that you are grand, and we will tell you more. This is a lifetime.

You cannot know it all now. Don't ever think this is the way it is to be. The small Truths must come before the grander Truths. Each small Truth *is* a grander Truth. You must just see it as so.

You are upset that we know all you are thinking and feeling. It is the way that we will help you. We can answer all your questions before you have asked them. Do not wish that this is not so. We are not of the human realm. We do not judge, so do not worry about what your soul has thought. It is right and it is good. Be glad, for we know your every wish.

You, too, know the answers to all your questions—all you have to do is remember them. Just know that you know. This is how our message will come to you: when you remember, we will tell you. *That's kind of cheating.* Why is it cheating? We will tell you All when you remember All. This is how things work here. Do not worry. You will remember. You are remembering more each day. Be patient. All will come. You are Love. You are Light. You act as Love would act. Continue this and you will know All. This is the Truth.

Live your life as a prophet, and you will be one. This is what you have prayed for, so this is what you will receive. You will be the greatest of messengers. We will tell you this many times because you still do not believe it. Believe it and you shall live it. Remember! You have done this before. Just as the Reiki symbols were placed in your hands centuries ago, so were the seeds of remembrance. Remember and it will be so.

Who is this? This is Da. You will not hear anyone else until you need someone else, and then you will create another. This is all *your* plan. This is God's Plan. You are One. His Plan is your plan and your plan is His. This is all of your own creation. You call us, but you think that we call you. It is you creating us to call you. If you truly did not want to come, we would not call. This is how God's Plan works. See? Small Truths, but Truths none the less.

Hear this grand Truth: you are in charge of your destiny. You have asked to become a great messenger, and so you shall be. This is the way it works: ask and you shall receive. Speak this to all. It will take some time for all to understand, but they will understand in time.

We are glad that you used your Reiki in front of the kids in your youth group today. Do not worry what others will think. Just do it! No one blinked an eye today. You are so comfortable with these kids. They understand. This is where you shall start: start with the kids. They have open minds. They are clean slates on which God can write His message. You will be the one holding the pencil. Write His messages of Love on their minds so that they will know the Love of God, and they will not be afraid to show it in public. As you do, they will do. Be the example of God's Love in the open, and they will follow. Know this and it shall happen. You have a very special group of kids. Love them and they will love you. Love them and they will love God. They will not be embarrassed to show their love for you or their love for God openly in public. This is how it is meant to be. Know this and be still.

You are getting tired. It is late. *Yes, I am.* This is where we will end for today. We are Love and you are Love. You are Light and we are Light. Walk in that Light. Follow that Love. Show Peace to all. This is our message for today.

Love always,

Da.

Now you may go to bed with a happy heart because you have known us, and you know we love you. Goodnight, my sweet child. Pleasant dreams. We love you.

November 29

You are here and we are here. This is good. Do you not know that this is good? You have come in love—love for us, love for your Self, and love for all others. This message is for all others. Send it out in the Glory of God for all to hear. You are the One—the chosen one to be our voice—to tell all of the Love of Jesus Christ. This will be your story. This will be your song—your song of Love. To know God is to love God. You have come in love and faith. This is what the others must do: come in love and in faith. You are so good. We know this and God knows this. We have been told of your goodness through the generations. You have come just as they have said you would.

You have come at just the right time to save the earth. This is a crucial time. So many resources have been used up, so many resources have been wasted, and so many things are used by so few people. This is not what God had in mind when He created you. This is not the way it was meant to be, but technology got ahead of itself. You wanted so much, so you invented it—all marvelous things—but you do not need them. You think they make your life easier, but they do not. Think about it. Why do you need dinner cooked in a flash? Why do you need round-the-clock entertainment on the television? Why do you need computers? At least you are using yours for some good, but we would have come without a computer. You do not need all these things. They make you hurry and they make you scurry. You need to work long hours so you can afford to buy them. Bigger—better—faster is your motto.

When I speak of *you*, I speak of your species. As humans, you have been driven to be better and to have more. You compete to win. Why? If you win, what do you get? *A trophy and the satisfaction of winning.* Another *thing*—and something that you should already have without competing. You do not need to compete. It makes you angry and sad when you do not win. You teach your children that winning is everything. It is not. You have won just by being you. God does not keep score. You are the only ones who do. Who gets paid more, who works more, who has more? These are the important things to humans, and it is why your world will fall. It will fall as sure as the stars fall from the Heavens and shoot off into a brilliant blaze. That is—if you do not stop.

Somehow you must show them your Light, and you must tell them that wanting and having are not important. They do not need, and they do not need to want. "Having" does not bring happiness. *And exactly who do you think is going to believe me? Not the "me" generation!* Ah, but there is where you are wrong. They know in their hearts that all this is not making them happy. They know that there is something else; they just don't know what it is.

This is what you shall do: tell them of the "something else." They are yearning for it. It will be grand. They will follow. You know them—once one does it, they all will want it. It will become the "in" thing. They will follow just like mice. They will follow you, for they will see your happiness, and they will want it. They need to have what you have.

But won't they want to take it from me in their need to compete? And how do you expect that they could take it from you? It is not something you can lose. Give it away. Give it all away, and there will be more. Do you not give love away and does it run out? No, there is more. Always more. There is more than enough happiness to go around. Teach your children not to want and not to need. This is the key to happiness. For what they want, they will never have; they will only know the wanting. Be happy with who you are, and this will bring you happiness.

You have a headache. *Yes, I do.* Well, wish it away.

What are you waiting for? You do not need a headache. Wish it away and it will go. After all, you created it.

You are still half-asleep. This is a good way to come to us. Your mind is still groggy and not ready to think. We will be able to speak more clearly to you without your mind being in the way. Listen to the music. It is the music of God. It is in your heart. It can never *not* be in your heart.

You are so good. You listen. You heed our messages and listen to your intuition. You come when we call, and you do not second-guess what we have said. There is no doubt in your heart that this is real, but you still doubt yourself. You do not doubt us, so do not doubt yourself. We will be with you.

I just don't think that anyone is going to want to read this. To the average person I think it would be too repetitious. Not for me, but for them. So many of the messages are personal. How will it make a difference to them? Because, my child, your story is their story. There are so many families who have gone through the same things as yours. There has been hurt and regret enough to fill the Heavens. So many people need something to grasp onto as real. They will believe. Keep preparing the book. We will help you write the inserts to the messages. You have the gift for writing. You write beautifully, as you speak. And this is because it comes from the heart. That is why what you say is so important. It comes from your heart, and people know this. They see this as genuine love. You do not worry about what is said, you say what is in your heart. Write the book this way, and people will know that you are genuine. They will flock to hear these messages.

Is it boring for you to hear the same things over and over? No. So why then would it be boring to them? They are searching, just as you are searching. They will find the same comfort you have. *But how will it be a comfort for them to hear all about how good I am, and how I will be a prophet?* Good question that time will show the answer to. This will start out about you, but it will not be all about you alone. It will be about all. It will be the way for all. You are just the messenger. It is your job to get it out to the people.

How long do I wait? When do I collect the messages and declare them a book? If truly these messages are to last a lifetime, how will I know? When the time is right, you will know. And there will be many books—not just one. There will be a lifetime of books; each written in the glory of God, each written to honor your Selves. You will learn. This is not the end of all things. You will learn, but you cannot waste any more time. The time is now. The world is ready. Keep typing and keep believing. That is all you need to know for now.

Send out the message verbally. Speak up to all who will listen. Tell them of your Great News: that Jesus Christ is born, and He is you. They will laugh, but then they will think. *What if they don't understand all that is spoken here? My daughter was very confused at the "We are God" statement.* Of course she was. Were you not the first time you read that statement? Do you understand that it took you over a year to understand and believe? And what made you really understand that the "God is you" statement was real; that it could be? *Your message about the Universal Spirit, the One Source coming down into us. That statement made me understand how it could be that we are God and He is us.* And this is how they will come to understand it. Do not worry. All is well.

They will understand—and if they don't—it is not your problem. Do not let the disgruntled opinions of some dampen your spirit. Some will discourage your beliefs. Some will call you blasphemous. Some will call you traitor. But some will call you Love and some will call you Light and some will call you Prophet and some will call you God. Do not judge your life or your message by what is said about you. Good or bad; it is your message and mission. There will always be judgment, but it is not to concern you. You are above all this. You know that it does not matter.

Do not doubt yourself. All is well.

This is going to be enough for today. We have learned much, and I can feel that you are becoming strong. You are thinking. You are asking good questions. We will give you all the answers. All you need to do is ask.

With love always,
Da and Us

November 30

You are here. This is good. We are glad that you have come when we called. To know you is to love you. This is the Truth. We are here just as you are here. We come in love, just as you do. We know why you are here. You want to learn more. You are so fascinated by your new life. You can hardly believe that this is happening, but you know that it is. You believe. We look forward to seeing you. This is how it is to be for eternity: you come and you learn.

This will be a lifetime of learning. You will never *not* be learning. We know how happy this has made you. It has given you something to look forward to each day. You come here with an open mind and an open heart. You do not question whether it is true; you know it to be. This is all that we ask: come with an open heart and listen. You will be our messenger—our messenger of God's Word. You know this now, and you are becoming calm. You can see how this is going to happen. A great number of things have been going on within your soul. You have come to know that all is true. You have come to accept our call. You will be our messenger. There is no doubt. You have begun to write the book. Keep writing. Do not wait until the end, or you will forget all that you are feeling and all that you have felt. This is what will make the book real—not only our messages, but also your thoughts and your feelings. This will make them know all is true. This is what we ask of you.

Do I ever have a choice? Do I ever get to say no? Of course you have a choice. You know this. This *is* your choice. Come on! Start from the beginning. This is all your creation. You know that. *But sometimes it seems that it is not me creating, but you who are telling me what to do.* That is your mind thinking. You know that it is not your mind that is in charge; it is your soul. Your soul is creating. This you know. Tell your mind to back off and let the soul do its work. This will be the mind's job: step out of the way and let the soul fly. When this is done, there will be no stopping you. You will be able to create the world as it should be. *Wow!* Wow is right! But it will happen. Your mind has given way so much already. It is the only way that you could hear us. You have a very strong soul. It is tired of being held back, and it wants out. It wants to fly and be all with the All-in-All. This is its true desire.

We will help your soul find its way. You will never be lost. This is what you must tell the others: let the soul have its way and you will never be lost. For if you were lost, God would find you just as the shepherd found the one lost little sheep. And you can never actually be lost anyway, for He is within you. You must know and you must tell: we will never leave you alone. We will be there in your comings and your goings. In the bright of the morning and in the dark of night, we will be there guiding you with our loving hands. Be still and feel our hands guiding you.

Look to us for the answers. All can get them. You are not the only one. You are not the only God. You are just here now before the others. There have been many before you, and there will be many after you. You will get many started on the spiritual path. You shall spark the interest, the wonder, and the amazement. You will help them know God. They want to know. They need to know. This is what you shall do: you shall be our earthly guide to help them find us. We will leave a map for you so that you can leave it for them. Do not fear. We will show you the way so that you can be the way for the others. *Beam me up, Scotty!* I know it sounds like science fiction. Some will see it as that, but some will not. This is the way it is meant to be.

Not all souls desire the same thing at the same time. Yours is an old soul. You have been at this for many, many, many centuries. Others are young souls, just beginning, just new. *Are there only a certain number of souls that are recycled over and over, or are there new souls created at different times?* Souls are created as energy gathers. When a large amount of energy gathers in one area it becomes a magnet, and draws in more and more energy. When the energy is blessed with God's Love, it literally bursts into being. It becomes One—One with each of its parts and One with God's Love. This is how new souls are created. Of course we recycle old souls, but the energy of new souls cannot help gathering and becoming One with God. It is the plan of the Universe. It is the way it is meant to be.

Where do all the souls go? Exactly where they want to. Some will stay with God in the All-in-All, and some will stay as guides and angels. Some will go to earth in the form of humans to learn, and others will go elsewhere to learn. *Where is the elsewhere?* The Universe, my child, the Universe. And not only the Universe as you have known it, but God's Universe. All is All, All is here and All is there. And All is not here and All is not there. It is All. All happening. All changing. All the same. The Divine Dichotomy.

You are here, but you are not here because you are there. You are there, but you are not there because you are everywhere. You are everywhere, but you are not everywhere because you are not here. It is a continuous circle. Time is not here. You are not here. You are everywhere, and time does not exist. It is all happening now. Right now. *I just still don't understand time.* You will, my child. We are not going to try to explain now. You have had enough lessons for today. It is time for me to leave. *No, please don't.* We know you feel so close to God when we speak, but you can learn only so much at one time.

Yes. Thank you. You are so patient with me, and you are so gentle. I feel that God is within me when we speak together. I know, my child, but you do not have to sit and type to feel me. Look into your heart, and I am there. We all are. We are One. Remember? *Yes.* We are One. I can never *not* be with you. Do not miss me, for I am not gone. Think of me, and you will know that I am there. I love you. We all love you.

Goodbye, my child. Walk in Peace. Walk in the Light. Walk in Love. Be still and know that I am always here. Do not miss me, for I am not gone. We love you. You are ours.

Love,

Da

The love that I feel is beginning to encompass my being—both mind and soul. The struggle is coming to an end. Even my mind is opening the door to believing that they are all within me. The gift is being accepted. All is becoming peace—complete peace.

The idea of writing a book still leaves me with mountains of doubt and a great number of unanswered questions. Transcribing messages is one thing, but putting into words all that I feel is entirely another. This project will take an incredible amount of time and work. Do I put all the work into it just to find that no one else is interested in a book of Heavenly messages? Da has just spoken as I write. He has told me to have faith. It is my journey. It is not reaching the goal, but what happens along the way that is important.

And so I will gather my dictionary, my thesaurus, and all the self-esteem that I can collect and write the book. My mind knows that there is no turning back, and my soul is pleased.

December 2

We are here. We knew that you would come. This is the story of all stories. Stay calm. You need not worry about what is to be said. This is Da. We are Light, we are Love, and we are soothing music. This will be our story. You are Light. You are Love. No need to fear, for God is with us. This is His story. He is Light and He is Love. These stories will be the comfort of your life forever. This you must know: this will be a lifetime of comfort. We are so glad that you have come.

You missed us yesterday, and we missed you. You were busy—too busy to hear us. *Is that bad?* No, it is not bad. There is no good or bad. It just "is." You were busy, so you could not come. We do not judge, and you should not judge yourself. It just "is." This is the way it is to be. *(Pause)* We are still here. No need to doubt. No need to fear. No doubt. No fear. This is how your life will be: calmness.

(No words were spoken for a while, however, I knew we were not done.) We are still here. Do not worry. Feel the music. *(Long pause, automatic typing. For the first time during automatic writing, the words are actually decipherable.)* kkkkkkkkdjthekslptlathisltkdko thatisloelhtslktklsal thatis ltovelyoudknowlov. ewiealkndowlove.tlheis thenothenednd dwa relwallthere you mustknowthat. This is how it is to be. We speak and you hear. No more. No less. This is how it is meant to be. We will try many different ways of communicating. Some will work; some will not. Do not hold judgment on them. Just let things be. We are with you. We will always be with you. No need to fear losing us. Even in the silence, you have not lost us. We are still here.

Calm down. You are anxious today. You are waiting. Do not wait. Waiting creates expectation. Have no expectation. Accept what happens and what does not. *You know me so well—what I am feeling and thinking.* That is because I am you. This is how I know. This is how we all know. *If this is so, then why don't we all feel the same at the same time? The saints and the murderers—how are our feelings different?* We are all different, but we are the same. The Divine Dichotomy.

I am feeling you because we are tuned into your energy. Our energy is at the same place. We are very close. It is what you call, "picking up someone's vibes." It doesn't matter how physically close or far away you are. It is how energetically close you are. You can pick up on Debbie's vibes, even though she is physically far away, but you won't have a clue as to what Larry is thinking, even though he is right there. Energetically speaking, you are on different planes. All planes are One, but we focus on some more than others. This is how it is. You must know and believe.

In times of what seems like aloneness, know that you are not alone. Be still and know that we are here. We are all with you spiritually. All is true. All is Truth. We are nothing but Truth. This is the Truth. There is no other way to be. To this be the end of all things. We are here for you. We can be whatever you need. If you need comfort, we are here. If you need spirit, we are here. If you need a warrior, we are here. We can be whatever you need. Please do not ever feel alone; you are not. We are here. *But sometimes I need someone who can help me understand all that is happening. This is hard to get from you.* In other words, you need confirmation from the human world that all is true. You need to hear a human tell you that he believes. Why is that? *Because I am human.* Oh, my child! You are so much more than that! You are more us than you are human. Your soul is gaining strength, and you are becoming more Spirit than human. You can rely on us. We will help you understand. We will help you believe.

Isn't it going to be hard for me to live in the human world when I am becoming more Spirit than human? Yes and no.

Yes—in relating to things and doing things and seeing what needs to be done and who needs what and where they need to be. This you will have more conflict with. But who you are and who they are and who the world is and who we are—this you will see clearly. You will find complete peace. And what is more important—what needs to be done or who you are? Think about it. We will never let you become so much Spirit that you lose your human side. We need your human side to get our message out.

When the message is done, you will become all Spirit, and you will be One with us as you cannot be as a human. That time will come, but there is much to be done in the meantime. You will be human for a long time. You will be grand. *I am worried about living up to all that you have told me.* Why? Create it and it will be so. Believe it and it will happen just as you planned it. Just as God planned it. Just as you both planned it. No need to have expectations—just "be." This is all that you must do: stop doing and just "be." This is the key to all: stop doing and just "be." Just "be."

Goodbye, my child. You will be great and grand and wonderful and beautiful and the Savior and the great I AM and you will be God. Walk in Love, my child.

Da and us

Having just placed the beginning pages of the manuscript in its cover, I have begun to understand that this is real. This is not something that is here today and gone tomorrow, as so many of my other whims have been. This is a commitment that will last a lifetime. I open the manuscript cover and it says, A Mother's Words ... Beyond the Grave. My mother gave the title to me and so I will keep it, although her words do not fill many of the pages. But then I am reminded of what Da has told me. It doesn't matter who is speaking, because they all carry the same message.

Even though my soul understood all that my mother had said, the human part of me was still having difficulty completely trusting her, and so I believe that she lovingly stepped out of the way to let Daniel come in and speak to me. And when I began to have difficulty hearing Daniel, he so lovingly stepped out of the way and gave me Damon. They all do carry the same message, and so the title is not incorrect. They still are a mother's words beyond the grave, but they are a mother's words spoken through the Oneness of the Angelic Realm.

December 3

We are here. This is what we ask of you: be true to yourself. You do not need to give your Self up to accomplish what you must. You can and must stay true to yourself. We will help. Be still and know God. We will always help you to know God. There will be times when it may seem that He is far away, but know that He is not. He is right where He always has been and always will be. He is in your heart. Listen to this message and keep it close.

We are Love. God is Love. You are Love. To this be the end of all Truth. We love you. You are the messenger. You will come and help the others. You must know this as true. *My ears are buzzing and I feel dizzy. Why is this?* It is we. You can hear us singing. You have always been able to hear, but you just thought that your ears were buzzing or ringing; you just did not know it was us. It is we. You are hearing us sing. *(Long pause)* We are still here. We are giving you time to relax and let go. You have been so busy that it is sometimes hard to relax and hear us. Take the time to relax. Do not let the silence disturb you; we are still here. *(Pause)* Listen to the music and let your heart flow with Love. This is our song.

See the Love in each and every one of you. Do not look for the faults—look for the Love. You are getting closer to Larry because you are doing this, and he is doing it also. He is ready. It is time now to tell him. *Could you come to him to help him understand and believe?* He must call us and create us in order for us to come. Do not take his skepticism on as your own. Be strong and do not be angered. He is not right and you are not wrong. He is just creating a different place than you are.

(Long pause) We are still here. Relax and listen to the music. You need to slow down. You are so tense again. You are doing too much—all in God's Name—but too much. Take care of yourself. Be good to yourself. *How do I know how much service is good? How do I know when it is too much? How can volunteering your time to help others be bad?* When it hurts you. Do not give so much that it hurts you. This is not what God has intended. Be selfish. Take care of yourself first. Help others after you have helped yourself.

What about all the things that would not be done in church? Then they will not be done. *What about all the children's programs? You said I was to help the children.* It is your way, but not at the expense of yourself. You do not have to make fifty quilts in order to help. You would help by making ten quilts.

(The youth ministry sews quilts and donates them to the Salvation Army. This year the kids made fifty quilts. This, along with the preparations for the Sunday School Christmas Program, had left me feeling exhausted.)

You do not have to take over everything. *Well, what about Sunday School? Sunday School would be gone had I not volunteered to take over as superintendent when no one else would come forward. Sunday School would have ceased to exist.* No, it wouldn't. Maybe it would not have been done as well as you do it, but it would have been done. They would not have let it go by the wayside. *Shouldn't things be done the best they can? Why settle for less than the best?* This is the perfectionist in you showing up. *I do an excellent job. Everyone knows that I put my heart into all I do.* Yes, you do, and it is at your own expense. We know what you are thinking, we do. *I know. Should I say it, or do you want to?* Go ahead. *If my name is on the project and if it isn't done just right, then what will people think of me?* Bingo! You are correct! Your mother told you this, and she was right. You are still so scared of not being good enough. You are better than you could ever imagine, and everyone knows that. They love you.

But don't they know I need a break? Why doesn't someone speak up and offer to help? You have created a situation in which no one will stand up and offer, for if they do then what would you do? You worry people will think less of you if you do not do everything. You like doing everything because it makes you feel important. You have not understood that you are important without running all those activities. Everyone knows this, but you. It's time that you know and own this idea. Create someone to take over the Sunday School and he or she will be there. You have created a place where they need you. Now create a place where there are others to help.

Get over the fact that no one does it as you do. Yes, you do things bigger and better than almost anyone else, but is that really necessary? *If you want things to work, yes.* Ah, but they will work even without the perfect set of circumstances. Step back and create that person or persons who will come in and take over. You also intimidate many people because you are too perfect at doing things. Step back and look at what is really important, and you will see just how much or little needs to be done to be a good volunteer of God.

Give, but do not give until it hurts. This is what you must do: do less yourself, but do more creating. Create it and it will be there. You have seen how this works. Be with us and you will be doing God's Work. Take time for yourself. You are grand without all the stuff. Go in peace, my child, and relax.   Da

Pondering this message I realize that there have been many people who have spoken up and offered to do small things. And so often I don't accept their offers, convincing myself that I will do the noble thing and not bother them, only to find out later that I resented having to do everything myself. Perhaps, indeed, it is because I am afraid they would do a less than perfect job—or even worse—they might be able to do it better than I could.

And then the miracle of all miracles happened. My mother touched another of my sisters in a new and wonderfully different way. And it was another new beginning.

My Butterfly Story

Written by my sister,
Shelly

It was a very cold and blustery December morning when I decided to go to my mother's gravesite to take her a Christmas wreath. I have felt the only place my mother would hear me talk to her was at her grave. I have come a long way in attaining my goals since my mother passed over, and my continual thought has been that I wished she were here to see what I have achieved.

After placing the wreath on her marker, I knelt down and began to cry, asking out loud, "Why did you have to go so soon? We had just started to get closer as mother and daughter, and you would now be so proud of all my accomplishments." Out of nowhere, a beautiful black and white butterfly flew right up to me, hovered at my hand for a few seconds, flew back and hovered again. I did not take my eyes off the butterfly, watching it disappear just as quickly as it appeared in front of my eyes.

I immediately became hysterical, sobbing like a baby. My mother's grave is placed on top of a hill in a wide open area. The wind was strong that day. There was no reason for a butterfly to be there in the dead of winter. I knew at that moment that it was my mother letting me know she has been with me, and has heard all I have said. This was also her way of preparing me for what my sister, Melinda, was about to tell me. My first thought was to run, but I didn't want her to think she scared me. I kept touching her marker hoping to let her know that I was not afraid—just a little freaked out.

The first person I thought of going to see was Melinda. This also was strange and out of the ordinary because Melinda and I had never been close through the years. If anything happened in my life, I would always talk to my friends before I would ever consider going to her. We never socialized together, and I never went to her house unless it was a holiday or one of her kids' birthdays.

While I drove, I was still sobbing and trying to get myself together, but stopping my crying just seemed impossible. Unfortunately, when I got to Melinda's house, there was no one home. It turned out to be a blessing because it gave me time to think about what had just happened, and quite honestly, I was still too upset to have been able to understand what she was about to tell me.

When I called Melinda later to tell her my story, she knew instantly that it was time to talk about mother, the angels, and the messages. After being visited by my butterfly, I had no doubt that what she was telling me was true. The grandest part of this experience is that Melinda and I have finally become sisters after all these years. We share everything. I call her if I have a problem, need someone to talk to, or just to say I love you.

So when you're talking to your loved ones who have passed over and something special or a little out of the ordinary happens, don't be afraid. It is just their way of showing you how much they love you, and letting you know that they will be with you always and forever.

Before I could even think, the words came tumbling out of my mouth rejoicing in their freedom. My marvelous journey was to be shared with another. And the fact that the other was my sister was a miracle! It would become the bond that would erase all the distance we had held between us throughout our lives.

Mom had prepared her with such an undeniable miracle—a winter butterfly, a sign of the resurrection—there was no choice for her but to believe.

December 4

Today was a special day. Today you are One with Shelly. She knows and she understands because your mother helped her to understand. The butterfly was your mother's Gift of Love for Shelly. The butterfly is the sign of the resurrection. It was a sign of her continuing life—a life that will never end. We are One. This is as it is to be.

Shelly has questioned in her mind if we would come to her. It is a question containing joy and fear. We will not come and speak to her unless she wishes it and creates it. Tell her to ask, and continually ask, and she shall receive. This she must know: this is a commitment. She cannot turn it off when she does not feel like being a part of it. Tell her to look at your messages. You have been so dedicated. You come when you are tired. You always come.

We will come to Shelly also, but she must know how it is to be. This is a lifetime. No doubt. No fear. No turning back. Not all are suited for this commitment. She must be sure and then ask continually. She cannot ask just once and have us appear. This must be continual prayer. This must be continual asking. Be sure she knows this. Tell her not to be discouraged if she asks, and we do not come. She may not be ready. Only we will know when the time is right. We are Love and we are Light. She is Love and she is Light. Tell her these things.

This is your mission of Love: be All to all. Be Love. Be Light. Seek Love. Seek Light. Act as Love would act. Act as Light would act. Be a beacon for Shelly to follow, a beacon for all to follow. You cannot fail. We are with you. You are so loved. You *know* you know. You say what has to be said in a way that shows love. We love you.

You must know this: we need your Love and your Light. Be still and know that we are here. This is your call. This is your mission: shine your Light so brightly that all will see the way. This is your call: be a Light for all to see. Go out into the world and shine your Light. This is your call: find the lost ones and bring them Home. We will help you. We will never leave you lost. You will always have the map to show you the way Home. The map is written in your heart. You will never lose it. You will never lose us.

You are beginning to believe. You are actually beginning to see the book written and in the hands of the world. You were so brave to tell Larry. We know how hard that was for you, and we were so proud that you did not judge him for his laughter. It may have been nervous laughter, but now he knows. Now he knows this is your life's work. Do not fear when people laugh. They will not laugh for long. See yourself on Oprah. (Yes, we knew that you had.) You cannot hide any desire from us. Let us know your fondest desire, and we will help you achieve it.

We ask that you use your creating only for good. Create so that the world can be a better place. Create a world of peace, a world of love, a world of equality, where all have and none want. Create it and it will be so. You will see it will happen. Know this: it will happen. You will be safe. We will not let harm come to you. We will keep you safe. This you must know.

Whoa, have I been rattling on! Any questions? *Hmmmmm—Why are pickles green? Whattttt? Where did that come from?* Who knows, but pickles are green because the creator in you made them that way. It is you who has decided that the pickle should be green. It was your plan. It is as it is, and as it always will be. Decide a pickle should be purple, and it will be. Just create it. You understand, but you still don't take creation totally into your heart. You must do this for all to be so. Take creation into your heart and make it real. This is as it is to be.

You are becoming more patient with yourself and with these messages. You are finding the small Truths that are really the grander Truths. Keep re-reading the messages and you will find them. They are everywhere. Do not *not* look everywhere. Look into every word. Every word is a clue. Every word tells all about us. It is time to get going. It is very late, and you need your rest.

Remember: give only until it feels good, and this conversation does feel good, doesn't it? *Yes. It feels like Love. It makes me so happy. It brings me to tears. I feel so close to all of you. How can this bond have happened in such a short time?* It has been a lifetime. This is forever, my child. Do not forget that this is a lifetime. We shall see you later. Go to sleep and dream of us. Ask us into your dreams, and we will tell you more.

Goodnight, my child, sleep tight. We love you.

Da

I am being taken for the ride of a lifetime on an emotional roller coaster, which neither slows nor stops. Unable even to catch my breath, I am taken to the heights of the journey—thrilled to be where I am. I understand and am living the message. And in the next second, screaming, I am plunged headfirst into the seeming reality of life.

I have read today's message so many times. It still amazes me that the angels know my every thought, my every fear, and my every hope. It is no wonder that they can easily get to the core of my problems. It is still my insecurity that makes me such an over-achiever. I fear that I will not be good enough because I have never been good enough. So often I think that I am over this, and now I realize that I am not.

December 5

We are here. Take some time to gather your thoughts. This has been a hectic day. We know it has been a wonderful day—a day of love and a day of reckoning for Shelly and for you. Now you are not alone. There is another who believes. Isn't that grand? Do not doubt the power of minds and souls joined in common creation. They are grand and powerful when they work together. This is the Truth. Your mother would not lie to you. *I am so glad that you are back.* I know that you are. You have been so full of love. You have been so honest with your sisters. I am so happy. Tell Shelly that I do know what has happened. I know you and your sisters have begun to become friends. I know also that you love me. Yes, this is all true.

This is the first time that you have had such a reaction to all of this. You are crying. You have been in such shock. It hasn't sunk in. You were becoming worried that you were not feeling the same emotions as the others. This is why: you are in the middle of the journey. It is so much for you. It has been a month of wonder and confusion. I can see that the confusion is fading, getting farther behind you. You are clear—clearer than ever before.

This is why you are here: to facilitate love and to help all to love better and more wisely and longer and harder so that they may be all that they can be. (Blow your nose.) I knew Shelly was ready—then and not before. I am not protecting her. I do not think that she is any more fragile than you or Debbie. She is strong, and she will be whatever she wishes. Love will come her way. She is not waiting. She has no expectations. With no expectations, she will never be disappointed. This is the way to live. Have no expectations, and you will never be disappointed.

The grand thing about being Spirit is that you can be here and you can be there and you can be everywhere. I can be with you and Debbie and Shelly all at the same time. This you must know: no playing the ends against the middle, no playing one of you against the other. It is all Love. That is all you need to know.

Tell Shelly this: Taylor is here with me. *(Taylor is Shelly's son who passed over when he was only one week old.)* Do not be sad, for he is not gone. He will always be with her. She will always be his mother. Know this and be still. *I am worried that this will all be too much for Shelly, and that all the old wounds will be opened up again.* This is a wound that has never closed. It is time to close it and move on. Taylor is here and he is there and he is everywhere. Shelly knows this. This will be a comfort to her and will make her strong. She is much stronger than you know. You must stop trying to take care of her and acting as though she is your baby. Let her grow up, and she will fly alongside of you, equal in all respects. This you must know: free her and she will fly.

Are you burdened with all this? *No, not really. It is just so much to understand. I am so glad that you have come back. I was afraid that you left me because I did not trust you.* No, my child, you must understand that you cannot hurt my feelings. There is nothing to hurt. This is how it is to be: you will learn from many of us. Sometimes I will be with you, and other times it will be another. You have enjoyed speaking with Da so much, but since this was about our family, I needed to come and speak this time. Da will wait for another time. He will be back. Have faith. We will all be back at one time or another. Do not be sad when one of us leaves and another comes. Be glad for each moment with each of us.

You are happy. You can feel your heart flying. This is good. You are bringing the messages to others by starting with your sisters. Do not be afraid to tell all. This will be the story. This is how it is to be. You told Larry and Shelly all in the same weekend. The earth has not stopped rotating, and the Heavens have not fallen. It will be okay. We will tell you when and who to tell. Ask and we will know who is ready. We know all who are ready. This is the Truth. We will keep you on the path to be with the right people.

Surround yourself with people of like mind. This will help your soul expand and grow. Your mind will take a back seat, and your soul will fly. Can you tell how much easier it is to hear me? Your soul is taking over. Your mind knows that it is time. We do not even need to call you. You come because your soul needs the connection. It needs to hear us. It makes you happy. It makes you fly. We are so proud. You have been a trouper, hanging in there and standing up for what you believe. Continue this and you will be a great messenger, as grand as they come. Do not fear. We know that you are becoming calm. We know that you are reaching for the understanding.

You are at the time of understanding when your human life still is long. You are so grand to be remembering now. You have so much to do. Do not fear for what is to be done. It will be done. It is God's Will. It is your Will. It is our Will. All are the same. All are One. There is no difference. This is how it is to be. We will tell you, and you shall pass it on and bring Light into a dark world. Feel what is in our hearts and you will soar. This is the Truth. We love you and you love us. God is here. He is smiling—just as you are. We are so happy and we are so proud. We are so glad that you are with us. You have no doubt. Be grand, for you are grand. Be still and know that you are grand.

We have done many things today; perhaps it is time to end. *Will you be back tomorrow?* If you wish, my child, I will. My love for you is so grand. You understand this. This is all that I could ask for. This is not the end of the life. There will never be an end. Know this and be still.

Goodnight, my child.

I love you.

Mom

I am so sad. Why—I do not know. This is my new life. It is a life full of happiness; a life where all is Love and Light, and yet I am so sad. Perhaps, it is only now that I am beginning to understand—to know exactly what my prayers have brought forth.

Mom unexpectedly showed up, and for the first time her words brought me to tears. Everyone seems to cry when they read the messages; everyone except me. I feel as though I have been standing behind a screen, allowing only small bits and pieces of me to come through to experience all that has happened. I don't understand why I feel this way. Perhaps, it is fear or perhaps, it is doubt. I should have neither, but this is big. It's so much bigger than I am. I feel so alone.

When the weekends arrive, my world is turned even more upside down. Hearing amid the commotion is impossible. And so I wait until the quiet of the night to hear these words. Now I am not only uncontrollably sad, but also exhausted and resentful. Love and Light appear to be so far away. The path is overgrown, and I am lost among the weeds. The map—where is the map? They said that I would never be lost because there would be a map. And then I realize the map is held within all my prayers. I have been so caught up in the journey I did not realize I had stopped praying. But God does not judge; He waits quietly for us to realize that all the peace and happiness that we are seeking lies within our prayers.

Although usually only God and I hear my prayers, I have decided to print them so that you may better understand my journey.

I sit down, light a candle and gaze into the eyes of Jesus Christ. The painting on my altar is so beautiful that it makes me feel close to God and so I pray:

Dear Lord,

I look to You for all the answers, and yet I know that You are looking to me for them. I know in my heart that I am God. I know in my heart that it is all here, and yet at times, it seems as if it is so far away. I thank You so much for what has happened. I thank You for giving my mother and my sisters back to me. I look at Your face and it is so beautiful. I must remember that it is my face also, and that I am beautiful because I am God. I do not have to feel guilty about saying that. It is so hard to believe that I am to follow in Your footsteps; to be like You. How can this be? It scares me, not in the sense of being afraid for my life, but more in the sense that I won't be able to fulfill these prophecies. You have big shoes. I don't want to take on the ills of the world. That's too big for me. I need to start small, but I don't know where to start. Could you please help me to know where to start? (I have just heard, "You have started.") I know I have. I have been told that this is a lifetime. I am so thankful that You are here always. I wish all could know the comfort of this experience, and yet not all could bear this. I am strong, and this is my desire. It is what I have prayed for, and I thank You. I thank You for being in my heart. Amen

December 6

We are here. We have been patiently waiting. This is our story. This is our song. We have been waiting for you to awaken to tell us that you love us. You have been asleep for so long. Do not feel bad that you have slept so late. This has been so much for you.

We love you. You love us. This we know. Do you know how much we love you? Yes, you do. We know that you know. This is how it works. You know love just as we do. You are listening, and this is Love. Do not fear, for we are always here. This is the Truth. Do you know this? Yes, you do. Do you believe it? Yes, you do. You have come to us with an open heart, and it is good. Be still and know God. He is with us also. He will never leave you. This you must know. Do you know this? Yes, you do.

You have learned much so quickly, and you will continue to learn. This you must know: you will never know it all. There will always be more to tell. Do not get bored with what is said. Do not be tired of hearing these things. We will say them again and again so you believe them; so others believe them. This is the way you learn: by hearing over and over again. You need not worry about how others will receive our message. This is not your concern. You deliver it; they will respond as they will. God will be with them. There is nothing that is too much when you understand that God is with you. Know this and be still.

You heard us singing to you earlier. As you were drifting off, your ears were ringing. This is no longer distressful to you because you know it is us. We like to let you know that we are here, and so we will sing. We are happy that you know it as song.

Please try not to let this get you down. You can celebrate. This is not too much for you. *I think I am only now beginning to understand.* Good. Your human form will take some time adjusting, but your soul is ready. It has been waiting forever for you to get to this point. Know that you are ready. Know that we are here. Know that you are Love. You will not falter. You will not fail. It is all right and it is meant to be. This is your wish.

I am not sure why I feel so sad and tired today. You will not feel this way for long. We will lift you up. *It seems that I am so sad on rainy days.* This is because you are Light, and Light loves Light. You see God in the sun, but you have a harder time finding Him when it is gray. You do not believe that He can still be here, but His Light does not go out; it is just hidden.

This is the way it is with all others. Their Lights are there; they did not go out. They are just hidden with stuff, stuff that makes them gray and covers their Light. It is easy for God to come through the gray because He knows His Light is still there. So many do not know this. They do not believe that they even have a Light, much let alone that it is grand. They are so in the gray that they have forgotten. Tell them the sun will shine. Tell them that their Light will shine. Tell them to come out of the gray. *But how, how do they come out of the gray?* Just as you. Come to God. Pray. Ask for help. Pray. Tell them that they must love God, and they must love themselves, for they are God. Without Love for yourself, you will always be in the gray. You will not know that your Light is there.

Help them love themselves for who they are. Do not judge and help others not to judge. You have done so well with this. You do not judge so often anymore. You are learning, and you have found your Light. Pass it on and let others know how you found it. Speak of God and His Love often. Speak of us often. *Won't people just think that I have become a Jesus freak? You know that turns many people off down here.* Yes, it does, when you spout it self-righteously. You must do it God-righteously. Put God first in all you say. Do not spout Scriptures. Do not preach. Show them by example. This is showing them God.

This is how you shall do it: live it—do not preach it. Anyone can preach, but not all can live it so easily. Succeed in living God's Words, and you will be passing on the

Scriptures to others without even speaking them. *But how will they know?* Oh, they will know! They have seen the change. This change has not happened just in the last month. It has been happening for years. It has been happening since you got out of your pew and began the work of God. The work of God is what is important. By giving of yourself, you are showing others the way to God.

So many people do not know how to give of themselves. They are afraid if they give it away, that there will be nothing left for them, but they are wrong. They do not know that there is always more. Love, Light, Giving, God's Will—give them away to all, and they will come back twice-fold to you. You will never run out. This you must know. This they must learn. Help them learn by example. Be a mentor to the world. Show them how it is to be.

Find people of like mind, gather in their consciousness, and it will grow and be grand. *Where do I find these people? How will I know?* They will find you, my child. Pray for time with Susan and her friends. Go to the healing circles. They will help you find people of like mind. They are everywhere!

Know that as you send out your Light, some will receive it. Use your intuition, and you will know who to tell. You can always ask us, and we will help you. You will find people of like mind and gravitate away from people who are not. Do not be afraid of this. *I am so worried about ending up alone. My friends at church are all that I have. They have been with me through all my times of trial, and they have shown me such love.* Yes, and some have shown you much distress. You have already distanced yourself from this. *You are correct about this, but is it right to distance yourself from the ones who need you most?* No, go out into the crowd of non-believers and do your work, but do not surround yourself with these people all the time for they shall drag you down. Be sure to be with people of the Light, too. They will recharge your batteries.

Do not forsake those who do not know their way, but

also do not forsake yourself by trying to help them find their way. You cannot make someone find his way. You cannot take hold of the reins and lead people. You may invite them to come. It is up to them to follow. *How much intervention do I use? How much do I do for them, and how much do they need to do for themselves?* Be there for them. Listen to them. Show them Love. Send them Love and Light. This is all you need to do. They will do the rest in their own time.

This has been a good day. You have gotten to ask many questions that have been on your mind. It is time that we leave. You must get up and get going. The day has begun without you. Be there in each day. Be there in each way. Be Love. Seek Love. Act as Love would act.

Love,
Mom

I am overcome by complete sorrow and see no way out. Why is all this not a comfort for me today? Why do I feel so burdened? I feel so dispirited and completely lost. Please help me.

Dear Lord,

I thank You for the gifts that I have received. Even though I do not understand why I am so sad, I know that there will be a time when I am not. I know that I am not alone. I know that You are with me, and I need not worry about being sad. It is just part of the process. I will not question it. I will be thankful for it. For to know happiness, I must know sadness. So today is a day of sadness. I pray for tomorrow to be a day of happiness. And even if it is not, I will not give up because I know that I am not alone. In the sadness, there is a sense of peace, a sense of peace in knowing that all is real. There is no more doubt that this is happening, and that it is real. I have been chosen, or I have chosen myself, to be the messenger. I will be that messenger. I will be faithful. Amen

PART THREE

The Journey Begins

The holiest of spots on earth is where an ancient hatred has become a present love.

A Course In Miracles

The Journey Begins

And at the end of every storm, there is a dawn, and that dawn has come to me. This will be a book. I can see that God has chosen me to bring these messages to you because I am a plain and simple person, living a plain and simple life, speaking in plain and simple language. I am just as you: a plain and simple soul who is ready to know God.

Today the messages have changed. They are no longer speaking to me; they are speaking to you. These are God's Words. Listen and you will know. He is speaking to you. He is the Way. Take His hand and follow. One hand. One heart. One soul.

December 7

This is your journey—your journey of Love. You have asked for it and you have received it. You are Spirit, just as we are. You are more Spirit than mind or body. Follow your soul, and you will find the key to happiness. It is not what you have or where you have been. It is your soul. It wants to show you All and to teach you to fly. This book has been placed in your hands by whatever means your soul could manipulate. It was your soul's desire to have this book, and so you do. Do you see how strong your soul is?

You are here in human form with mind and body, but it is the Spirit that is your heart and soul. It is the grandest part of you. All the rest is covering for the soul so that it may live in the human realm. Here we need no covering, so our Light shines brightly. We are Light—flashes of Light. You have seen us out of the corner of your eye. You think something is there, but when you look, it is not there. Know we are with you.

Free your mind from doubt, and we will come to you.

Call us in prayer, not once, not twice, but continually, and it will happen. Be close to your God. Offer yourself to the Lord. I know that it sounds scary, but give yourself to Him, and you will be with Him. This is how it is to be. Hear these words, and know that your God is near. He will never forsake you. He will be with you forever. Even when you do not know it, He is there. In your comings and your goings, in the morning and in the night, in your joy and in your sadness, He is there. He is so glad you have come here to read and learn. This is His book. This is our book. This is your book. We are One. This you must know: you are me and I am you and God is us. We are all a collective Spirit, and that Spirit is God. This you must know and this you must believe.

We are here to help you. Do not doubt and have no fear. If you let us, we will wipe them away. This is how it is to be: you come, and we wipe you clean. Come to us for this and know that you are pure in heart.

And now we must speak about controlling your thoughts. This will take some dedication, but if you let it, the soul can control the mind. This will be your mission for today: let your soul control your mind in little things. Don't worry about the big things; they will come. Pick just one thing: being angry, judging, swearing, or something else. Pick one thing and try to see "it" through God's Love. Do not worry about being perfect; you need not be. Love yourself for who you are now. Do not wait to love yourself until you are perfect. It will never come. Love yourself now. It is your way to God.

Be with Him in prayer. Say Grace and mean it. Not just words, but a blessing for the food which He has placed on your table. Yes, He has placed it on your table. You think that it has been you, but it has not. He has done it. He has helped you through your days so that food is on your table. So bless Him and mean it. Take a moment in the car, at those red lights that you hate so much, to say a blessing.

Thank God for the few moments that you do not need to think about driving the car. Take time at work to say a blessing also; just a thought, not a formal blessing, not a formal prayer. This is all you need. Thank God for being where you are at the exact moment that you are.

Listen for Him in your soul, and it will tell you much. It will tell you all you need to find the way. Listen to your gut feeling, that feeling that tells you to skip work a few minutes early to see your kids. Give them a hug. Give them a hug from God. Yes, you are God—so give them a hug. The children need to know your Love. Know this and be still.

Take time to help someone by giving of yourself. You will feel a glowing inside your heart and soul. As you look into the faces of the ones you have helped, you will see God and they will know God. It will give them hope for the future of mankind. This is what you must do: love all people of all circumstances because, "there but by the grace of God go I." Know this: this could be you. Do not judge their sadness. Do not judge their loneliness. Do not judge their addictions. Do not judge their circumstances. Do not judge their decisions. They are here because it is their path—their path to Me—their path to you.

You are Me and I am you. This is God. It is God speaking to you. It is you—speaking to you. This is not new. You know in your soul that all I say is true. You know this because you are God. And God would never judge and God would never condemn and God would never leave. This is what you know in the heart of your soul. Be still and know God. Be still and know your Self. This is your job for today: take time to pray and to know your Self. Thank your Self for the day's blessings.

Do not let the darkness overcome your life. When darkness comes and you cannot find your Light, ask Archangel Michael to shine His Light so that you may find your Light again. Do not doubt that it is there. It always has been, and it always will be. This you must know. This you must trust. This you must see. You are Light. All of you, who you really are, is nothing but Light.

It is skin and bones and muscle that are keeping your Light safe, but the Light is there inside—always. Be it in your heart or in your soul; it is there. Look for it. This is your mission: look for your Light. Look for the good in yourself. For unless you can see good in yourself, you will never be able to see it in others. Love yourself, and you will love others. Accept yourself unconditionally, and you will accept others unconditionally. This is the Truth. This is the Way.

You have been searching for the way. Follow Me and I will guide you, but you must follow. I will ask you to come, but you must follow in your own name. There will be no pulling and no dragging here. You must come of your own will, but know that if you do not choose (and you are choosing) to come today—I will be here every day, every second of every day, giving you the same offer. Follow Me to your soul. I will never *not* be there. This is as it is to be. I will offer, and you will choose to follow. It is your time. You would not be reading this book if it were not time to follow. Follow Me. You have nothing to lose and All to gain. Come to the All-in-All. Come to Me. Come to your Self. You will be amazed at how grand you are.

It is not too late. No matter what has happened it is never too late, for life shall never end. If there is no end, there is no time. Without time, there can be no end. Believe this, my child, and you will know All. My hand is outstretched to you. Feel it, take it, and come. Come with Me to the Heaven of your heart. Come and find your Self. Come and find Me. Take the steps one at a time and follow Me. One foot before the other. One thankful thought before one negative thought. One hand. One heart. One soul. This is us. One hand. One heart. One Soul. This you must know. Come. Come to Me.

December 8

This is our story. This is our song. We are One. This you must know: you have been placed on earth because it is your soul's desire to know itself through living. You must live in order for the soul to experience life. It cannot experience life as Spirit; it needs human form. Your soul has a plan. You must know this and understand. This is why your life has been what it is. It is your soul's desire to experience life. Your soul must experience pain in order to know joy; it must experience sadness in order to know happiness; and it must experience loneliness in order to know togetherness. Everything that happens is the soul's desire. This is the soul's journey: to experience what it is not so that it may know who it really is.

There are no bad things in life. Each is a learning lesson for the soul. It must experience until it understands, and when it understands, only then it will know who it really is, and so will you. This will be the moment of enlightenment. There will be no worries or sorrow; only joy, for your soul will know exactly who it is. It does not come easily or quickly. Lifetimes and lifetimes of experiencing are needed for the soul to learn. This is as it is to be. This is the soul's journey.

You are on a journey with that soul. It is impossible not to be on the same journey. The soul is the heart of you. It is the All-in-All of you. It is the part that is God. We are all here to know God, for God is within each of us. And we must know Him in order to know our Selves. We love you. We love each of you. You are us and we are you. It can never *not* be this way. Know this and be still.

In the depths of despair and in the moments of rage, know that we are here. As you do things that are considered wrong, know that they are not wrong. It is your soul learning. Do not regret what has passed through your life. It was your soul learning. There is nothing that you have ever done wrong. God understands and knows that this is the soul. You do not have to worry about eternal condemnation for what you call your sins. There is no hell. There is no devil. There is only Love. This is all you need to know. Do not fret over things that have happened. They have happened for a reason, and that reason is for the soul.

The time is coming for mass enlightenment. It is why the world is in so much trouble. It is the dark before the dawn. At this time the entire world is experiencing things that the soul does not want to be. The newspapers and the television all are full of crime, hate, war, and sadness. This is because so many are experiencing what they do not want to be. Do not worry how bad things will get. The entire consciousness of the world will change. It is coming. All will know that this is not what they want to be. All will know what they truly are. All will know Who they truly are. This time is coming. Do not worry about the future. The future is now, and it is grand.

This is our story. This is how it will be. When we love all people, there will be peace. All wars will be gone, for all will be Love. There is no other way. Do not have fear. It is always darkest before the dawn. We are all here to be saved by the soul. Know this and be still.

December 9

This is God's story. Come and we shall tell All. And so it shall begin. We are here and we are there and we are everywhere. This is how it is for us. We are not confined by a human form. We are Light. We can be all places at once. This you must believe: we can be with you and with everyone else in all places at all times. We are Light. Light can zing from one corner of the Universe to the other in a flash. Yes, a flash!

There are no constraints of time here. We are on parallel time planes. Time is not on our plane, but time is there for you on earth, and so we must relate to it so that you can understand. But understand: there is no time. Blink and we will have already been there. Think and we shall know before the thought is finished. We are with you. This you must know: all the Spirits are here and they are there and they are everywhere. They may be in human form, but because there is no time they can be with you in spirit form also. You are never alone.

We are in the stars and we are in your thoughts and many of us are in your life over and over again. Yes, souls do come back; of course they do. They keep coming back until they have learned their lessons. And so your loved ones come back, many times as someone else in your life. They are here in the spirit world, but they are also there in the human world. All is possible. This you must know. This you must believe: there is no end.

Your life shall never end. Please believe, for if you do you will never again fear death. And if your loved ones believe, never again will they grieve when you are gone, for they will know that you are not gone. They will know that you are alive, and they will look for you. They will look for you in their hearts, and if they look hard enough, you will come to them. You will come in spirit form as a guide or you will come in human life or you will come to them in another way. This is the way of the soul. The soul does not want to stay confined in the body any longer than necessary. Your physical death is its new beginning. So fear death no more. It is not the end.

Do not cry when loved ones leave their mortal form. Do not grieve, for they are not gone. In a blink, they can be there. All you need to do is ask. Not once, not twice, but continually, for when we know that you are asking with sincerity, then we will come. But know when you call us, you must listen. When you call us and invite us into your life, it is a partnership. What we ask of you, you shall do. This is how it is. We will come, but you must follow.

Today is a day of great revelation to you. You know the Truth. God is alive, and He is alive in you. Know this and be still. We are all you and you are all us. We are all one continuing circle. All energy. All in one place and all in all places. Energy blasts that bump into each other, mingle, and become One. It is the Universal Energy that is God. All is Energy. All is Light. A soul is created when the energy in one place becomes so strong and so intense that it calls to the Universal Energy, which is God. When it is blessed by God, it bursts into being. This is a new soul. New souls are created all the time, and a new soul has so much to learn.

Old souls have been here for many, many centuries through eons of time, learning their lessons, and coming to their enlightenment. There are many old souls in your world today, many old souls that have come to the point of enlightenment. They have learned many lessons, and they are ready to understand. It is the understanding of Me which brings enlightenment, not the understanding of the Bible, and not the understanding of the church, but the understanding of Me. I am the One you shall know, for to know Me is to know your Self. This belief will bring you Home and to understanding the All-in-All. It is there. It is within your reach. Take these words to heart and believe them. You will come to understand.

It is your time. Leave your earthly possessions and thoughts behind and come fly with us. You will know freedom and love like you have never known before. There will be peace in your heart. Just come, and let your soul fly. This is its true desire: to fly, to become One with the All-in-All, to become One with you; to become One with God. Release all that you are and all that you have and become who you really are. You are Light, and you shine brightly. Bring your Light to all that you see. Let it out so that all may see you for who you really are—God.

Shine and fly. This is the way to understand. Be with us, and you shall fly. You will know each of us by name, and we shall know you, for you are Me and I am you. Call us. Be with us, and we will be with you. This is the way to peace. This is the way to happiness. This is the way to understanding. This is the way to God. Come, for we are waiting—waiting for you.

One heart. One mind. One Spirit. One.

December 10

We are One. One in the Spirit of God. You, I, and all. We are One. So it is to be as it is to be. We are here to help you become who you are. When you ask, we will come to you. We will always be there. You may not hear us, you may not see us, but be assured, we are there.

You have been One with us, and now you shall invite all to become One with us. You can do it. It is in your heart. All you have to do is believe in the Spirit of God. Believe in the Spirit of your Self, and you will be One with us. No more hurt. No more fear. No more hopes. No more expectations. This is what you must do to be One with us: give them all up. Find *you*—amid all the garbage of life. You are there. You are just lost among all the possessions and all the places to be and all the things to do. You are there. We will help you find your Self. Know this and be still.

This is a journey that will last your lifetime. Take each moment one at a time. Step back and enjoy the ride. And a ride it will be. You will be lifted to the heights of exaltation, and you will feel as low as the mines of Egypt, but know in all this—we are there. It is a long journey, but you will not be alone. This is all you need to know: you will not be alone. Take whomever you wish with you. You need not go by yourself.

In the beginning, you may wish to be alone. Do not feel guilty if this happens. It is you finding you. You are so busy in finding you that you do not wish to do anything else. This is okay. Take care of yourself, but do not neglect the spirits of the ones that you love. They are on their journey, too. Be kind to them, but be kind to yourself also.

You must love yourself before you can love them. For until you love yourself, you will not know true Love. Believe this: you must love yourself first. These are our words. Hear them and believe: when you love who you are, you will not judge others. This is why you judge: you do not love yourself for who you are. You look to see if you can find someone who is less in your eyes so that you can feel more worthwhile. We all need to love ourselves, not for our physical looks, but for who we really are.

The Spirit has chosen this container, this body, in order to learn the lessons we need to learn. Humility, strength, love, kindness, compassion: these are the lessons that we are here to learn. Fear, hate, anger, criticism, and guilt—the soul will go through these things in order to learn what it needs to know. For without sadness, you will not know joy. Without criticism, you will not know compassion. Without hate, you will not know love. Know this and be still. You will need to learn who you are not before you can learn who you are. This is the soul's way of learning.

You are a container for the soul to learn—nothing more than a container. If you allow it, the soul will be in control. Do not let the mind and rationale get in the way of the soul. Do not question. Take your natural instinct, your intuition, and follow. Do not worry about what others think. They will come in their time.

You are here now. It is your time. Know this and be still. We are here to help you on your way. You will never be alone. Take our hands and follow. Do not be afraid, for there is nothing to fear. God is your rock, your defender, and your fortress. He will protect you from your enemies.

So do not fear, for you will be with the All-in-All. This we know as surely as the sun will rise and the moon will wax. You will be with us. You cannot be anywhere else but with us. It is your time.

All you have to do is take our hand. We will lead you to the All-in-All. We know the way. So do you. You have always known the way. We are One. You are Me and I am you. We are all One. We are all God. You know the way to God is through your own heart. It is through your own spirit. Go now, for we are waiting for you.

December 11

This is our message for today: you are Love. This you must know: know us and you will know Love. Take us into your hearts. Breathe us in as you listen for our Heavenly music. Breathe in the Love of all the angels. We are here. Breathe us in. You will know that we are near by the happiness that you feel. You will not know why, but you will be happy. There will be a peace in your heart, and you will feel calm. This is how you will know that we are with you. Feel the calmness. Feel the peace. We have given it to you as a gift—a gift from God. Take it. It is yours. We are Love and you are Love. This you must know: we have come to tell you All. Listen to our words and believe.

You will learn All, if you listen and believe. Each time you read our words, you will know something new and something wonderful. We will be with you always. This you must know: we will comfort you in times of sorrow, and we will celebrate with you in times of joy. We will never leave you, for you are ours. This you must know: you are one of us. This is how it is, and how it has always been. To this be the end of all things. You are ours. Take this to heart and be still.

We will come to you. All you need to do is ask—and

like a flash—we will be there. Look for us. Know that we are there. It is not too late. It will never be too late. No matter what has happened or what you have done or who you have been, you need not fear. We do not judge the soul. We do not judge you. You are Love and you are Light, and this is how it always is. To the core of your being, you are Love and you are Light. No matter what you do, you will always be Love and Light. Know this and be still.

Even if you have committed murder, you are still a creature of perfection. This you must know: your soul does things so that it can learn. Each soul has known these things in one life or another. We have all murdered, we have all pillaged, and we have all plundered. Every soul has done these things in order to learn what it is not. Each soul must experience what it is not, in order to figure out what it is.

With love and hope, you will have learned in the next or the next or the next lifetime that this is not who you are. You are not a murderer, you are not a thief, and you are not a cheater. But to know that you are not these things, you must have been them. Your soul has been here many times to learn—to learn what it is not so that it may know what it is. This you must know: do not judge the ones who have done wrong in your eyes. They are learning. This you must know: an eye for an eye is not God's Way. God's Way is Love and Light. Speak this Truth to all you see: you are Love and Light, just as God. Forgive. Forgive. Forgive. This is the Way.

Judge not and you will not be judged. Forgive, and you will be forgiven. Let others learn so that you may learn. This is the Way—the way to God.

December 12

You come to us for our words—our words of wisdom. Listen, for you shall hear many. This is how you wish it to be. In wisdom, we tell you that all create their own lives. It is you who is creating all that happens to you. You feel as though you are a pawn in everyone else's life, but you are not. You are your own creator.

You have created all that has happened in your life so that the soul could learn. Yes, you have created all the things that have happened to you. I know this is hard to believe, but you have. You have decided what your soul was to learn in this life, and you created it. It is hard for you to believe this because so many of you have created lives of hardships and sadness. Do not despair. For you to know happiness and safety, you must first know hardship and sadness. This is your soul learning. You must go through all that is hard, in order for it all to be easy. You are through the hard part. You have come to this book. You have learned. Your soul is ready to move on. Know this and be still.

You can be happy. You can be rejoicing. Your soul has learned, and now you can move on. This is how it is meant to be: your soul learns, and then it moves on. The move is always closer to God. It is always closer to your Self, for you are God. Know this: your soul will always move closer to God. It wants to know God, and it wants to know it Self. And for it to know it Self, it must experience itself as all, so that it may finally experience itself as the All-in-All. It wants to experience itself as God. It needs to experience it Self as God. This is what it is here to do. This is its journey.

When you understand the journey of the soul, you need not be sad and you need not fear, for your soul will take you only where you want to go. This you must know: trust your soul. It knows the way. All you need is the courage to follow it. Many times it is headed in places that you have not been before. Know that it only wants the highest experience for you. Trust that it will take you to the All-in-All. There may be many detours. Cherish each one, for the destination is not important. It is the journey. The journey is where all things of importance will happen. It is where the soul will learn. Love your journey, for it is yours, and you have created it.

You and your soul have created each circumstance in your life in order to learn. When you have learned through one circumstance—create another. When you have learned that work is not the most important thing in your life, create the time to spend with family and friends. All you must do is change your mind and create again. Create whatever you need. Believe it is there, and it will be. This is all that you need to do. Believe you have it, and you will.

It is in the wanting, that you will never experience having. For when you want, you think and believe that you do not have. Believe that you already have, and you will. You will not want, for you already have. Believe you have enough money, and you will. Believe you have enough time, and you will. Believe you have enough faith, and you will. Believe you love all, and you will. Believe you are God, and you will be. It is as simple as that. You are creating every aspect of your life.

When you find what you have created is not what you want, *choose again*. Create what you really want. All you need to do is to believe, but you must believe with all your heart. You cannot use this as lip service. You cannot say one thing and believe another. You must believe with all your heart. Believe and it shall be. You are as powerful as all that. You are God. This you must believe: believe and create.

Create a world of peace. Create a world where there is no hunger. Create a world where every child has a loving parent. Do not fall into the trap of thinking that one cannot do it. Do not feel overwhelmed or fearful. There are so many of you. If each of us creates it, how can it not happen? Keep creating. Keep believing. Know that it will happen. Believe. Know and believe. Have no doubt. For if you doubt, there is the tiniest part of you that does not believe. All of yourself, every fiber of your body and soul and mind must believe. Convince your mind to believe.

This is your mission: go out into the world and create. Create all that you need and create all that the world needs. This is your mission. Know that you will not be alone. We will be with you. There are many of us and there are many of you. When we work together to create a world of love, miracles will happen. Know this and be still.

December 13

This you must know: we are glad that you have come with us for the journey of your life—for the journey of your soul. This is as it should be. This is as it has been for the eons of time. This you must know: we are here to guide you on your way to your Self—on your way to God. He is waiting for you to know yourself as Him. This is all that He asks: know yourself as Him.

Do not worry that some will think that this is blasphemy; it is not. Anyone who thinks this does not know the way to Me yet. We are here for you today, for you are ready to know yourself as One with the All-in-All. This is your Truth. You have come with an open heart and an open mind. You are ready. Do not fear what others will say. This is your journey. You are on your path. Allow others to walk their path so that you may walk yours. This is the way it is to be. Allow others so that you may allow yourself. Do not judge others so that you do not have to judge yourself. Love others so that you can love yourself. This is the journey.

We have been watching and waiting for you to come.

We have been watching your Light grow stronger. It is getting brighter. The Love in your heart is growing. Do you feel it growing? Your heart is glowing with God's Love and Light. We all have the Light, but you have found yours, and All is rejoicing. We have known you, and now you know us.

You can rejoice in the knowing that all is just as it should be. All is in place for you to come to us. Know this and be still. This will be our journey. Take all who wish to come along. Tell all who will listen. Many are ready. This is the way you can save the earth. Tell all who will listen and bring them along to know us. Do not be discouraged if they do not come. Do not be sad. Do not be angered. Do not judge. It is not their time. Their path will bring them to us when it is time. This you must know: you may lead, but you cannot drag them along. This you must know: speak to all who will listen about the Love that you know, but do not despair if they do not follow. They will come when they are ready, just as you have. We are here to all who wish to find us. This you must know: seek and ye shall find. Ask and it shall be answered. These are words of Truth.

This will be your song—your song of Love. Listen and you shall hear it. You shall hear it in the ringing of your ears. You shall hear it in the singing of the birds. You shall hear it in the cry of a newborn baby. You shall hear it in the songs of Christmas. This is as it has always been. We have been singing to you; you have just not heard. In all the simple joys of life, know that we are there. Listen in the spring breeze and in the roar of the winter wind. We are there.

When you know we are with you, you will never feel alone again. Do not worry if you do not know us fully yet. You are learning. It takes time. You have all the time in the world. You have an entire life, and many more after that. It will come to you. You must just be patient. We have come to tell you that we love you, and that you are one of us. This is what you need to know: you are One with us. We are One. This is Truth.

You will come to know us and to know your Self, as well as to know God, for we are One and the same. You cannot know one without knowing the other. We are One. You are Me and I am you and we are God. He is not a large figure up in the Heavens. He is with you. Do not think of God as someone "out there." He is not someone who is keeping tabs on all that you have done. There is no gate where Peter stands with his Book of Sins. There is no such thing!

Know this and be still: you can do no wrong! Whatever you have done has been your path. God does not condemn. You cannot go to hell, for there is no hell. It has been made up in order to keep you in line; in order to bring you closer to God, but it has not brought you closer to Him. It has made you fear Him. This is not His plan. He does not need you to fear Him. He wants you to love Him. He is not a vengeful God, full of wrath and hate for those who appear to do wrong. There is no wrong. This you must know.

God is Love and God is Light. If you believe in God, you can never go to hell. But if you believe there is a hell and you create it, you will condemn yourself forever. It will not be God, but you who have put yourself in the everlasting fires. For if you create a hell, there will be one; but know that it is not there unless you create it. God is Love and understands all our paths. You do not need to go to hell unless you wish. Do not create it and it will not be there. It is as simple as that.

Know that you are Love, and that God accepts all who search for Him. You are with Him in this life and the next and the next and the next, for it never ends. It goes on and on. Know and believe that life does not end. It will never end. It cannot end. You will be with us for eternity. Fear nothing, for we are with you. This is as it is to be.

Love, honor, and cherish God and yourself, for you are

One. This will be the Sacred Trust: love yourself and love God; honor yourself and honor God; cherish yourself and cherish God. These are your vows. This is the way to know your Self and God. This is for what you have been searching, and so this is what you will find. Know this and be still: we are here. We can never *not* be here. You will never be alone again. Feel the Love in your heart, and we will be there.

You are One of us. You will always be One of us. You have our peace in your heart. You have our love in your life. Be happy. All will see it in your eyes. They will know that something is different. They will know that you are happy.

Spread this happiness to all who wish to receive it. Tell them of your love for God. Tell them of your love for your Self. This is what you must do: you will be our messenger. Just as the messenger has brought this book to you, you must take these words out into the world. Spread them among all who wish to listen. You are Love and you are Light. Speak and they shall listen. Be a messenger on your own path. We do not ask more of you than you are ready to give. Be our messenger. It is the way to the Lord. It is the way to you. Be still and know that all is well. All is just as it is to be.

Come to us and bring all who wish to follow. Come, for we are waiting. Bring one or bring thousands. There is room for all. Know this and be still. You are a great Light, and you have so much Love in your heart. You would not be here, if it were not your path. All is just as it should be.

This is your story. This is your song. Get ready to tell and sing. Come fly with us. Let your spirit soar, and you will know the happiness of the Heavens. All will sing, for they will know that you are here. All will rejoice, for they will know that you are God. All will follow, for they will know that you are the Way. Come to us. Be with us. We are here for you. *For you.* This is the way to the Peace and the

Love and the Happiness. Do not doubt. Do not fear. This is the Way. This we ask in the name of the Lord. Amen

December 14

You have come this day to know us—to know our Love and our Light—to find your Love and your Light. There will be many times when you will not be sure our Light is there, but know that it is. We would never leave you alone. This you must know: we will always be with you. My name is Sam. I will be with you, and we will learn. This is the Truth. It is not Da; it is I. I have come to bring you the Truth and to tell you of the Love. We are all here, but it is my turn to speak. I love you. I will always love you. This you must know.

We will be here for you, whenever you are ready to learn. Pick up the book and find the Truths. Pick up the book and find the Love. It is right here—right here before you. All you have to do is seek. Seek and you shall find. We will take you to places that you have never been. We will take you to your heart—to the Heaven of your heart, for Heaven is in your heart. It is within your reach.

Heaven is not a place you go when you have died, for you cannot die. Heaven is where you can go to feel safe. Right now. Heaven is in your heart. This you must know: all the Peace and Love and Light is right there—right there in your heart. Just feel it. It is there. You need not wait until the time is right. Do it now. Right now. Feel the Heaven of your heart. Stop and listen to your heart, and it will speak to you. It knows All, and it is waiting for you to know All. It will wait until you are ready. Know this and be still.

Your mind is like a sponge. It will absorb all the information it can so that the soul can process it and learn. Be careful what you put in your mind. If you put garbage in, then garbage will come out. This you must know: be pure in thought and mind. You need not be perfect, but you must do your best. Be pure in thought, word, and deed. Think only highest thoughts. These are the thoughts that will lift you higher to know God. Stop the swearing. It does no good. It is only used to shock people, and to emphasize what already has been said. Speak in a language of Love, and you will not need all those words. Put only pure thoughts in your mind so that only pure words will come out of your mouth.

Be careful what you watch on television, in the news, and in movies. If violence and hate enter your mind, this is what will enter your heart. Your heart will be cold, and so accustomed to seeing violence that it will not be shocked anymore. It will become part of the fabric of your life. It will become part of your heart. You do not need to witness any violence—real or fake. It is not good. It is good to be pure in thought and in mind. Put only Love in your mind, and only Love will be in your heart.

Take care of yourself. You are the container for the soul. This you must know: the container is mortal. It will not last. The soul will go on forever, but the container will perish. Take care of your container. Eat only the foods that are pure, whole, and clean. This shall keep the container healthy so that the spirit can be here to learn its lessons. Do not use mind-altering substances. They do nothing for the heart, but are for the mind only. The drugs, the alcohol, the cigarettes, the chocolate, the soda, the coffee—the chemicals—they do nothing for the heart. They trick the mind into not feeling. The mind does not want to feel, for it is so hurt. It does not know how to cope with all that goes on in life, and so it escapes through these things. They do nothing for your heart or for your spirit. They only allow the mind to escape.

Your mind need not escape when you know God. Your mind will gladly stay to witness the Love. It will welcome the presence of the Lord. It will take some time to convince the mind that you need not have these things. The mind is strong, but the soul is stronger. Give in to your soul, and your mind will become compliant. Be pure in thought, mind, and spirit. Help your container stay healthy. Let it live so that the soul can learn its lessons. You can do it. Look to us. Look to the Heaven of your heart. We are there.

This you must believe: you can be pure in thought, mind, and spirit. You can be pure. Take away all that is not pure, and all that is left is Love—God's Love, our Love, and your Love. Our Love is One. This you must know: we are One. What you do for yourself, you have done for all. Be One. Know that you are not alone. Be One with all of us. We are here, so you need not fear. Listen to the wind and feel us in your heart. We will make you strong. Believe and you can be All.

December 15

This you must know: we are Love and we are Light. Be with us in all that you are. This is what we ask. You are Love and you are Light. We love you. All will be clear when we are done. At the end of your mortal life, All will be clear. You shall return to us in the All-in-All. This is how it is to be.

We love you. God loves you. You can love yourself. We do not lie, so you shall know this as Truth. You are good. We have come to tell you this so that you know you are worthy of our messages and our Love. You are so worthy that it makes us sing. Listen for us, and you will hear the voices of the angels. They are not human voices. We sing in the sounds of nature and in the sounds of your mind. When your ears ring, it is us. We are singing to you. Know this as us, and you will be comforted. Know this as us, and you will be happy.

You will love all, just as you will love yourself. You will love all as brothers and sisters. The world will be One. It is a grand vision that we have for the earth. All will be One. All will know. This is your mission. This is your song: be One with all on earth. Do not judge. Do not hate. Do not damage. Do not fear. There should be no fear in your life. You know that all is happening because your soul wishes it. This should be a comfort to you. There is nothing to fear. We are there. We are with you.

Today's message will be grand. Love all for who they are. This you can do. It will take some adjusting, but it is not hard. See the ones that drive you crazy—through the eyes of Love. They act this way because they are finding out who they are not. This is the soul's way of learning. Do not fault them for this, but let them learn where they feel safe.

You will be a messenger to all. Make them feel safe, and they will listen. They will hunger for all you have to say. They will know that you know All, and they, too, will want to know. Tell them, and if they laugh, do not despair. It is not their time. Do not fear persecution for all you know. You are safe. We will be with you. This is as it is to be. You will know you are a messenger when you see the Love in the faces of all. All will learn. Eventually, all will learn.

Change the world with your smile. Do not frown. Smile. Everyone will know that you are God's ray of sunshine. They will know this by your smile. Be happy and pass it on. Just as we have passed Love to you, pass it to them. Then they will know our Love also. This is as it is to be.

We have come to tell you about us. We are Light. We have no feet. We are streaks of Light. This you must know: you shall see us from time to time. You see something out of the corner of your eye, but when you look we are gone. We are with you. Feel the energy in the air, and you will know we have been there. This can happen to you. Just ask … and ask continually. Invite us into your life, but know

119

that when we are there, you will not be able to ignore us. This is a Commitment of Love. To know us as Light on earth is a Commitment of Love. Ask continually in prayer, and when you are ready—we will come. This is how it is to be. Ask and you shall receive.

December 17

We love you. You are an incredible creature—full of Love and Light. This you must know. This you must believe: you are incredible. You are! You are so full of goodness that it makes our hearts sing. We sing for the Love of God—for the Love of you. This is our song. This is your song. We have been watching. You are changing. We have seen. You have changed little things. You have been aligning yourself with God and with the Light. This is so wonderful. You are aligning yourself with us. We welcome you with open hearts and open arms. Your life will never be the same. It will be full of wonder, amazement, and happiness, for you know God.

This has been our mission: to help you know God and to help you seek God. It is only the beginning of your life. We have only scratched the surface. There is so much more for us to tell you. We will tell you All when the time is right. Know this and do not become impatient. You will hear the same messages over and over until they become ingrained into your heart, and until your mind believes them. We will say them over and over until you believe. Then, and only then, will we tell you more. Be patient. We have all the time in the world.

You are Love and you are Light. You are beginning to believe this. We want you to believe; to know that you are pure Light—pure Light radiating out from us. This is as it should be. You are a single ray of Light that radiates into the Heavens for all to see. We can see you. Your Light is shining brighter and farther. You were a little glow, and now you are shining brightly. This is how it will be: your Light will shine brightly to call all others.

You shall call them and tell them of the Love of God—of the Love of God for them. You are not the only one who has the Light. Each person has the Light. You are no more special than anyone else. You are special because you have found your Light, and you have come to us, but know that all can find their Light and come to us. It will happen in their own time. This you must know: you are all special in God's eyes. This is how it is to be. Feel special, but know that you are no more special than anyone else.

All will be with us; it is only a matter of time. Time will come and time will go. This you must know: there is no time. You are all here now. You all know All now; you just don't know that you know. There will come a time when all will know at once that you know All. This will be a time of grandness. It will be the time when all prophecies will be fulfilled. This will happen. The time is coming. More are finding their Light. The earth is not doomed. Do not fear for your children and grandchildren. You are learning. The earth is learning. It will not be doomed. All will be saved in a flash of Light. In a flash—all will know and all will be saved. This is all that you must know: all are learning.

This is me. It is Da. I have come to tell you of the love for music, soothing music. Listen to music that soothes the soul. Listen to the music of the Heavens. Listen to it and let it take you away. Let it bring you closer to us. Let your mind become entangled with the music so that your soul can sneak away to fly. It is the grandest thing to watch your soul fly. Become One with the music. Rock. Sway. This will engage the mind. The mind wants to let go so that the soul can fly, but it is not sure how to do it. Become One with the music, and your mind will let go.

Listen to music as you meditate. It is not hard to meditate. Sit in the music, quiet your mind, and know that all is well. Sit in your quiet mind and listen to the music. As your mind drifts to thinking, and it will, gently bring it back to the music. This is all that meditation is. Light a candle for God and ponder about nothing. With closed eyes, see the colors and the pictures behind your eyes and in your mind. This is all that meditation is. Know that you and God are One. Be One with the experience—whatever happens. Do not judge your experience. Do not judge your mind. Do not judge yourself. All is well. The experience will be exactly as it should be. How can it not be? You have created it. It is exactly what you need at this exact moment. Be grateful for whatever has happened. We are all here to help you on your journey.

Call on us frequently. Call us by our names. Call us as One Entity. It matters not. Call us and we will be with you. This you must know: we are here to be with you—to help you through your journey to us. This is our mission: to be Love and Light to you so that you may know Love and Light, and so that you may find your own Love and Light. We ask that you learn these things. All we ask in return is your thanks. Thank God for sending us to you. Thank yourself for bringing us to you. You have created us. You are God.

Create us to be with you. It is in your hands. It is in your soul. Create us and we will be there. We will never leave you alone. This you must know: you will never be alone. You will never be alone. You will never be alone.

December 18

We are here. This you must know. It is easy to listen to what we say, for you know that it is true. We love you. You believe this. You are Love. You believe this. Now believe this—you are God! He is you and you are Him. This is the Truth. You have read our words, and you know that it is us.

This will be a great help to you in your daily life. You have the strength of many behind you. You shall never feel alone again. This you know as true.

We have come to speak to you through this book so that you may know yourself as God. This is not a day's or a month's or even a year's journey; this is a lifetime's journey. You have been so good to come here and read our words. This will be one of the most important books that you will ever read. It will change your life, and it will change the life of the earth.

You have come here with your heart open, willing to accept all that we are giving. Be sure to pass what you have been given on to others. Do not worry that they will not believe. Do not worry about appearing foolish. You can never appear foolish to anyone but yourself. You need not worry about whether others believe. The others will come when it is time.

Speak of us and watch how it affects others. You will know that they believe because you will see them change. It will happen right before your very eyes. They will be different. They will be in their own Light. They will know that they are in it, and it will change them. This is your mission: you shall help change the world. You will not be alone. Many are ready to change. Many are ready to give up the old outdated beliefs and come to us. The earth is ready. Speak the Truths, and they will come.

The millennium is ending, and it is time. You have come to us to enter the new Age of Aquarius. You will enter it with eyes wide open and see All. None shall get by you. You shall see All. You shall know who is ready and who is not. In the twinkling of an eye, you will know. Seek out others with the twinkle of God's Love in their eyes. The Light will shine through that twinkle, and you will know that their heart is filled with Love. This is whom you must seek out. Seek out the Light. Gather together and make your Light shine as One. This is the way it is to be. Shine your Light so brightly that all will see and come to you. You shall attract others with your Light, and their Lights will shine with yours. This you must know. This you must believe: they will know you by the twinkle in your eyes. Look for the twinkle. Look for the Love. It is there, and it is grand.

The Love within your heart is growing strong. You are beginning to accept people for who they are. You are becoming more confident in yourself, and so judging is not as important. Feel good about yourself, and you will not need to judge. You will feel the lightness in your heart, for Love weighs nothing, and yet it weighs all. It is free to give away, and yet it is the most expensive thing that you can give. You can give it all away, and it is still there. This is how Love is. It is All, and yet it is nothing.

Love is so grand. When you give it away, it only grows. Your heart and soul expand with all the Love you have given away. Love all, not just your own. Love your neighbors and love those who anger you. Love your enemies and love your family. Love all whom your eyes gaze upon. Love all who enter your thoughts. Give Love to the guy who has just cut you off in traffic. Give Love to the person who is complaining in the supermarket. Give Love to the child who has just made fun of your child. Give Love to your family, even when they anger you.

Whatever you give away comes back as a mirror to you. When you give Love away, it mirrors Love back to you. If you give anger away, it is you whom it will affect much more than the person you are directing it toward. You are a mirror. What you give out comes right back to you. Make your life a shining mirror—a mirror that shows Love and Peace and Calmness and Understanding.

Forgive yourself when you do not mirror what is the highest for you. You are human, and you are learning. When you mirror what you do not wish, forgive yourself. It will be okay. Each time you mirror Love instead of anger, the soul will learn. One step at a time. That is all you must do: take just one step at a time. This is how it is to be. You will falter and you will triumph. It is the way that you are to learn. Be gentle with yourself. Do not expect to be perfect. You will have imperfections sent into your life so that you may learn that you can live with them. They are God's gift to you. Learn to live and love those imperfections, and you will learn to live and love your own imperfections.

Do not expect perfection. It is not there. It is not meant to be there. Have no expectations. This is the way to peace and happiness. If you expect nothing, you will never be disappointed. Take life as it comes and be grateful, for all that happens has been called into your life by you so you may learn. This is the purpose of all things: to learn, for the soul wants to become One with us.

Do not regret anything that has happened. It has happened for a purpose, and that purpose is to know us, to know God, and to know your Self. Everything that happens is for a reason. There is a lesson. It is there. You will learn if you look. Ask for help if you cannot see the lesson, and we will help you. Never fear that all is lost. You can never be lost. Your human life with all its triumphs and tragedies has been placed here by you so that you may come to us. Celebrate all the moments of your life and look for the lesson. It is there. Just quiet your mind and look.

You shall see it among the lines and spaces of your life. Your life is a book that you are writing day by day. You write the lines. You plan the scenes. You know the outcome of each and every day. Once you know and believe this and take it into your heart, your life will change, for you will know that your life is not a random act of God. It is you. It is you deciding what your life will be. It is you choosing all the circumstances and all the outcomes. Know this and you will change your life. Pray for your life to be what you wish. Pray that you will be who you are. Pray and create your life. You can have the life that you wish.

December 20

To know you is to love you, and so we shall always wait for you. This is how it is to be. There are many of us waiting for you because we know that you will come. You are on your way. It is the beginning of your journey; your journey to us, your journey to your Self. We have been here for many years waiting for the time to come for you to know us. We have waited patiently, and now you must wait patiently for us to tell you All. All is within your reach. Do not search frantically, or you will push it away. Wait patiently, and it will come to you.

Pray and wait patiently. Pray for each and every one of God's creations. Pray for the protection of all. Pray for the understanding that the earth is a precious creation of God, and that all must protect it. Pray that the resources of your great earth shall be shared by many because they know that this is God's creation, and it should be cherished and treasured.

Do not kill even the fly, for the fly is God's creation also. The fly is always in your face wanting to say "hello" for he is friendly. The fly is one of God's friendliest creations. He does not judge. He comes to say "hello." Do not kill any of God's creations. Each has a place on your earth. Each is worthy of learning its lesson.

Share with all who need. The earth needs to know there is plenty for all. For those who have plenty do not need all they have. Share what you have that is extra. Take what you need to live and give the rest away. Share and the world will have enough for everyone. This is the way to know God.

Food, clothing, and money are things that you need to live. Live—but do not lavish yourself with any of these. Take what you need and pass the rest on to someone who does not have. Share the world's resources with countries that do not have them. Those with oil—share. Those with food—share. Those with the technology to save the earth—share. Become One with all nations. You are not separate. How could I be One with you and not One with them? For if I am One with you, and I am One with them, then you are One with them also. We are all brothers. Learn this lesson soon. We are not separate. We are One.

What you do for others—you do for yourself. Help them and you will help yourself. Give away some of what you do not need. Do this often enough, and you will affect the collective consciousness of the world. Your thoughts and actions are sent out as vibrations into the world of energy. You are not the only one knowing what you are thinking and doing. Your thoughts will be picked up by others, and when their energy combines with yours on a thought, it is sent out into the sea of energy larger than it was before. When someone else picks up the energy and makes it his own, the thought or idea becomes even larger—even larger and harder to ignore. It becomes so massive that more and more people will pick up the energy and do likewise. This is known as the collective consciousness.

You do have the power to affect others, even though you are only one. This is because you are the One. The only One. The very One. The All-in-All. Know this and you will know your power. You have the power to change the world. Take a long hard look at your planet and think about what you can do to make it better. Pick one thing and do it well. Put your energy out there for all to pick up and make their own. This shall be the way to save the earth.

December 21

We are here. This is as it is to be. We will share with you the lessons of the angels, the lessons of the Light, and the lessons of God. These are your lessons—your lessons of the heart.

We shall come to teach, to share, and to be with you. We will give you strength when you are weak. We will give you hope when there is none. We will give you happiness when you are sad. All you must do is to let us into your life. All this can and will be yours. You are a child of God—a child of the Heavens. You are pure Light which has been blessed with God's Love. We have come to tell you all you need to know to find your way back to us. It is a path that will become well-journeyed, for many are on their way.

The new millennium is almost upon us. The Age of Aquarius is here. Get ready for great things to happen. The world will sparkle once again before the new millennium is over. It will shine like one of God's jewels. It will be a long path, and a path of many lessons. There are many ready to start on their journey. They need not go alone. This they will know: we will be with them every step of the way. We will be there. So many will know of us, and so many will believe. This is as it should be. This is as it will be. The dawn is coming. Know this and be still.

We are here to guide you to that dawn. The dawn will be brilliant, for each and everyone's Light will be there. It will be all the Light coming from all of God's people that will make the dawn appear. Do not look to the sun to know that it is dawn. Feel it in your heart. Feel your Light grow.

The dawn of the new age is in you. Yes, you! You will bring the Light to the world. You will bring all the Joy and Happiness into the world. You will bring Peace and Love, and you will bring the Light of the new dawn. It is not hopeless. The earth will not perish. You will bring the new dawning to the earth. It is within your reach. Put love for all of God's people in your heart, and the earth shall not perish. Be responsible for giving up what you do not need to those who do, and you will bring the dawn. Be Love to all, and you will bring the dawn. Be Love. Seek Love. Act as Love would act.

All will know that this is true. There will no longer be those who do not believe. They will be washed in the Love and the Light, and they will be pure. No more crime and no more hate, no more sadness and no more pain. It will all be washed away in the dawning.

It is coming. Do not fear. You shall be here for the new dawning. Do not worry that you will miss it. You will not. You will be the one in the middle with your Light shining brightly. You may not look as you do now, but you will be there. The essence, the soul, the heart will go on forever. It is waiting for the new dawn. Have no fear, for you will be there.

December 22

This is how it should be: you love us and we love you. This you must know: we love you and are here to guide you to us. You have been lost in so many ways. So many tragedies have come into your life. Some of you have lost love, and some have lost children. Some of you have lost jobs, and some of you have felt like you have lost your sanity. Many of you have just lost yourselves. You have been lost among the trials of life. You have been lost in your work, in your possessions, and in your addictions. You have done anything so that you would not have to be with yourself. This has been a pattern you have followed for lifetimes.

You have run away, fleeing all that has been, but have not known where to go. Do not run away. Cherish each and every moment, for it is what has brought you here. Your soul has been learning. You have not gone through all the misery and sadness for nothing. It has all happened for a reason. Your life has not been wasted. No matter what has passed, it has not been wasted. Your soul has been learning all the lessons so that it could come to us. Do not be sad for all that has passed. It is not too late to forgive all that has happened. This you must know: it is never too late. You may go to all who have hurt you and give out your heart to them. Even if they have passed on to another lifetime as I have, you can still make amends.

Forgive all for what has happened. If you have been wronged, it was for the purpose of your soul and the soul of the person who wronged you. Whatever has happened; has happened for a reason, and that reason was to learn and to know. Make amends with all those with whom you have had troubles. They need to hear you say that you understand, and so do you. For when you forgive someone who has wronged you, you forgive yourself.

You feel that each thing in life that happens is partly your doing, and you are right. It is your doing. You have created each and every circumstance in order for your soul to learn. Your soul, as well as the soul of the one who has hurt you, have made the agreement that this should happen just for the purpose of learning. Both souls needed to learn, and so they made a pact. Each would learn by this experience. To know joy, you must know hurt. To know happiness, you must know sadness. The soul knows this, and so it looks for the sadness, and it looks for the hurt. It knows this, and so it is willing to go through what it has to in order to learn. For when it learns, then it knows. The more it knows the more it will learn.

Speak out all your hurts, in a loving way, to all whom you need to tell. Let them know that it is okay and that it was meant to be this way, but that it does not have to be this way anymore, for you have learned and you know. You know the ways of Love. Love those who have hurt you, and you will know Love to the highest degree. Forgive and forget. Do not ever hold anything over their heads—ever. This is not the way. Forget and understand. For to understand is to know that all is calm, and that all is meant to be.

All is exactly as it was meant to be. You called everyone into your life in order to learn. Love them forever, for they have given you the greatest gift—the gift of understanding. It is time to know us. It is time to know your Self. It is time to know God. Now is the time. Come, for we are waiting.

December 25

On this holiest of days, we are here. We will always be here in all your triumphs and all your failures, in all your trials and tribulations; we will be here. Know this and be still. Jesus knew this, and that is why he was not afraid. He was never afraid of what the prophecies had foretold. He knew what was to be, for he had created it. He and his soul created all that was to be, even before the Child was born.

This you must know: Jesus' soul was learning, just as yours is. He was no different from you. He was just as you are today. He was not afraid because He knew us. He understood that this was what His soul had asked to experience so that He could understand His own Eternal Life. He knew this, and so He was never afraid. He was not afraid as He hanged dying on the cross. He knew that He was not alone. He knew this and was still. He knew all that was to happen, and yet He was never afraid, for He knew that there is no such thing as death. He knew that He would triumph over death and live forever.

This you must know: there is no fear. Jesus knew and believed. Please, now you must know and believe. You can feel safe just as Jesus did while he was on the cross. He could have saved Himself and yet He chose not to because this was His soul's highest desire—His soul's need to learn. This He knew, and so He was not afraid. Live your life without fear. When you are not afraid, you will live in the Light, and you will know the silence that comes when your heart is happy. We came to Jesus, and we have come to you. Know us and be not afraid.

For to know us is to know peace in your heart and in your soul and in your mind. Know us and you will know peace. Your life shall be as calm as the surface of a pond on a day when there is no wind. This is the calmness of knowing God. This is the calmness of knowing us. Know this and you will be calm.

There will be calmness and peace in all that you know and all that you do. Even when there is no peace around you, you shall know calmness and peace, for this is what is in your heart. This shall be our gift to you. You shall know that this is our gift by the calmness you feel, and by the peace that you know. This is our gift—our Christmas gift and our gift of everyday. Just pick it up, and live it. We are with you.

We have come today to send you the Love of Jesus Christ. He was born so that the world would know about Eternal Love. Pattern your life after Jesus Christ, and you shall have all the Love that He was sent to bring. This was His mission: to bring Love into the world and to bring the hope of Eternal Life. This was His mission. He came and He lived and He died and He rose—all so that you shall know Love. This was His Mission.

This is your mission: believe in Eternal Life and in Eternal Love and in Hope and in Peace. This will be your mission: live your life as Christ did—with Love, with Light, with Hope, with Peace, and with Joy. Let Christ be your Guiding Star. Invite Him into your life, and you shall be inviting all that you ever need to know into your life. This is as it is to be.

Blessed Christmas. Know Jesus and you will know All. Look up and follow His Star. The journey is long, and yet not so long. The journey is hard, and yet not so hard. Your life shall be a journey to God. Your life shall be a journey so that you may know your Self for who you really are—God. Enjoy the journey. This is your life's work.

December 26

We are here. Read this book and take to heart all that is said. It is all Truth. You will learn, and you will find your way Home—to us—to your Self. You will find your way. My name is George, and I am here to help you. You will need a guide through all that is to come. I will be only one of them. There will be many. We will come and go—all in the name of God, all in the name of learning, all in the name of Love. We will come, one by one, to help you. We may identify ourselves or we may not. It need not matter who is here.

We all carry the same message—the message of Hope and the message of Love. It is within all of our hearts and souls. It matters not who brings the message. It will be the same. You will come to know many of us. We will speak to you through this book until the time is right for you to call us. We shall come to you when you call. Know this and be still: we are within each of your hearts and souls. We can come to you. It matters not how you learn; it matters only that you learn of the Love and the Hope and the Peace and the Joy. This is all that matters.

Do not worry about learning All. This you must know: it will take time, but you will learn. Take all that we say to heart, and you will learn. We will be with each of you every moment of every day. We will be there. You will never be alone. Feel us in your heart, and we are there. Believe and it shall be. This is all that you need to know: believe and it will be true. This book has been placed in your hands at exactly the right time. You have called this book into your possession. Do not worry or wonder how it has happened. All will happen when it is time, and it is time. Know this and be still.

We are kind and loving creatures—kind in heart, and loving in soul. Know this and be still. We are creatures of the Light. This you must know: we are pure Light. We are pure energy radiating out from God—pure Light that is God. You are that pure Light also—in human form. The power of the mind and of the soul is miraculous. You can be anything that you wish. You can be anywhere that you wish. Know you are there, and there you will be. Believe you have it, and you will. Use the power of your creative abilities. Create and you shall have all and be all that you wish. Believe you have, and you will.

Love is all around you. It is everywhere. It is so often hidden in the desperation and the need of people. It is hidden in self-consciousness and in self-doubt. It is hidden in prejudices and hate, but it is there. Love is everywhere. Know this and you will see it. Give Love to all, and you will see more of the Love that is around you. You can affect many with your Gift of Love. For when you give Love, you shall receive it. You can affect many with your Love. Show Love and acceptance to all, and what you shall receive in return will be Love and acceptance. Know this and be still. There is so much hurt in your world that Love is hidden. It is pushed down so deep, and so you think that Love is gone. You believe it has to be gone for you to feel so bad.

Begin to smile and feel peace, even when there is no peace, and the Love will begin to surface. Feel calmness when there is no calmness, and you will feel the Love grow. Feel the acceptance of all people, even as the thoughts of prejudice cloud your mind, and the Love will rise up into your heart. Accept all, love all, honor all, and cherish all. Know that all is well, and the Love will come.

Begin by loving yourself. You must love yourself unconditionally before you can love others. Accept yourself for who you are, and then you will begin to accept others unconditionally for who they are. Do not worry about being perfect. It is all just as it is meant to be. This is God's Way, for all is perfect in His sight. Let all be perfect in your sight. Let all be perfect—flaws and all. All is just as it is

134

meant to be. This you must know: accept all that is in your life as perfect, for it has a purpose, and that purpose is learning.

Hear the music of your soul. Your soul wishes to speak out the joy that it is feeling, and so it will sing. Listen for the music. Listen for the Love. The music may come in many ways. It may be a sound, or it may be a feeling. It may come in the form of a friend or of a book or of a gift. It may be a poem or a flower. It may be in the sun or in the moon. It may be in the kiss of a child or the caress of a lover. It may be in the wind or in the rain. It could be anywhere.

The music of your soul is not necessarily music as you know it. Listen to your heart, and you will know when it is singing. You will have a sense of peace which will tell you all is well, that you could leave your earthly form this very minute and be happy. You will know that all is well, and that you have had the happiest life ever. When you feel peace—even for a moment—it is your heart and soul singing. Listen for the music. Feel the Love. Feel the happiness. It is there.

Relax and let go of all that troubles you. Let go of all your fears. Let go of all your expectations. Let go of your human life. Let go, fly to us, and you will know the Peace and the Love of Heaven right here on earth. Show good will and kindness to all, and you shall know Peace. Share the wealth of love, and you shall find the Love. It is there. It will not be hidden for long. You will feel the Love rising in your soul. Do not be afraid to let it out. Let the Love grow until it encompasses your whole being. Let your Light shine out for all to see, and they will know that you are Love. Show Love to all, and they will learn to let their Love grow. They will let down their guard, and they will begin to feel. For when you let your Love out, all will know that it is safe—safe to love, safe to feel. Let your Light become a beacon for all. Let them know that it is safe. Let them know that it is God calling them. You can be so much more than you are right now. You are coming to know who you are, and you are coming to know just how grand you are.

Knowledge is the way. Understanding is the way. Love is the way. Show all the Way. Do not worry if you do not know the way Home yet. It will come—and when it does—be prepared to bring all who are ready. Pass your message of Love to all so that all may find their way just as you are. Do not worry about where you are on the path at this moment. You will not be left behind. We know that you are here. Do not worry you will be lost. You will find your way. You cannot help but find your way, for we are guiding you. You will not be lost, for we have found you, and you are ours. This you must know and this you must take to your heart: you are ours. Come into the Oneness and be with us.

The soul is the grandest part of creation, for it lives forever. Know this as Truth, and you will know your grandeur. We are here to help you know just how grand you are. Let us show you the way. Do not hurry and do not worry. There is plenty of time. God knows you, and He will not leave you behind.

December 27

You have come to us because you are ready to hear our Heavenly message. This is how it has always been meant to be. This is your highest desire: to know us as we know you. You have come to learn and to be lifted to the heights of exaltation, for you know happiness lies where we dwell.

This is our story, and it will be your story. You are brought to this life to learn, and the learning will never end. It will continue for lifetimes until you know All. We have said this before and shall say it many times more—all so that you can know and believe. This is how it is to be.

Take the time you need to learn your lessons. There is no hurry. There shall never be a need to hurry. You have all the time in the world. You need to stop and take time to breathe, to smell the flowers, to listen—really listen to your loved ones. You need to stop and take the time. For in your world time will go, and when it passes, things will change. The children will be grown, and you will wish for the time that you did not take while they were young. Stop running them around, and take the time to listen to them—really listen. Be there in the moment—not thinking about the next thing to be done. Listen, for you shall be amazed at all they have to say. They need your time. It is the most valuable gift you can give to them.

Most of today's children are starved for attention, time from their parents that is theirs—without work, without friends, and without the phone. They need their own time—time that is not their sister's or their brother's. Time to talk to you about all that is important to them, even if it seems unimportant to you. If it is important to them, then it should be important to you. They are God's most valuable gift.

The gift of a new soul is the most precious thing that can be given to you. Cherish it and help it on its way to learning all that it needs to learn. But know that whatever happens, it is the way that it was meant to be. Your children have chosen you. Yes, chosen you to learn whatever lessons they need to learn. Your souls have come together in the agreement. There are no mistakes when you raise a child. Know this and be still. You have made no mistakes. No matter how badly you think you have done, you have done exactly as it was meant to be.

I am here to tell you what is in every mother's heart. Be it that she has passed over, or be it that she is still on the earth with you—cherish your mother. She has borne so much heartache for you. She has taken on all the burdens of raising your soul, and she fears that she has made mistakes. Go to her and tell her that she has done no wrong. All was done exactly as it was meant to be.

To all the mothers: know that you have done well. You have raised your babies to learn their lessons. You have done a good job. Let go of the guilt, fearing that you have made mistakes. Let go of that guilt for it does you no good. For centuries mothers have carried all the guilt and happily taken all the blame, for they think that it is theirs.

There is no blame, for all is just as it was meant to be. Know this and forgive yourself for whatever mistakes you think you have made. Forgive yourself. This is as it is to be. In order to forgive others, you must first forgive yourself. To forgive, you must first know forgiveness. You must forgive yourself for whatever you think you have done wrong.

Do not live in the past. Live in the moment. Live in the Now. It is the only way to really live. You cannot do anything about your past. Forgive and move on. Learn your lessons and move forward. Worry not about the past or about tomorrow. Live for now only. All else will take care of itself. Know this and be still.

December 28

This is our story, and it will be yours. You are Love and we are Love. You shall know this to the core of your being. You are Love—Pure Love. This is all that you can be. You can be nothing else. This is as it is to be. All are Pure Love.

There is only good; there is no evil. All is pure and all is good. This you must know and you must believe: the world is searching for a way to show its goodness. Many are coming to the time of goodness. The world shall know them as One. They will come together, and the world will live on. All are coming to the Light—and the Light will save all. Your Light will be among the others, shining brightly, so brightly. You will know that you are Pure Love by the way your Light shines. All will know you for your goodness. Your soul will have learned, and you will radiate God's Pure Goodness.

All are good; some just don't know that they are yet. The world is filled with souls who feel that they are worthless. It is not the soul that has told them this, but it is the mind. So many feel like failures, for they do not know that what appear to be their mistakes are just learnings of the soul. The soul knows that you are not a failure, but the mind does not. So many feel alone, for the mind tells them that they are alone, but the soul knows that it can never be alone. The soul knows that we are there, but the mind does not understand. Let the soul help the mind understand. The soul knows only goodness, success, and Oneness. The soul knows these things to be Truth. Believe these things also, and you will help the mind understand and become One with the soul.

You will never be alone. Look to the Heavens, and you will know that you are not alone. Count the stars on a moonlit night. Count the birds as they fly in the sunshine. Count the leaves as they fall from the trees on an autumn afternoon. Count the snowflakes that fall like the tears of angels. We are here. We will always be here—above, below, and all around. You will never be alone. We will be guiding and supporting you with the Love of God—with the love of your Self. Love yourself, and you shall love God. Be who you are—who you really are. Do not worry about what others will think. Be who you are in this very moment. This moment is the best moment of your life. This moment and the next and the next; each is the best. Live it that way.

Do not concern yourself with what people will think. Those who do not know will always talk. They will understand in their own time. Let them be themselves, as you want to be yourself. Do not condemn them for who they are. It is not for you to decide who they are. Let them live their lives in this moment and the next. Let them live and learn so that they may know also.

We have come to tell you these things so that you may prepare yourself for all that is to be. Ready yourself, for the time is coming for you to know. Release all that is judgmental, release all that is prejudice, and release all that is who you are not. Then you will be ready to know just who you really are.

December 29

And so the story continues—your life is your journey. Follow your life, and it will take you where you need to go. Follow your life, and you will arrive just where you need to be. The road is long. Do not let times of doubt throw you off your journey. Enjoy the journey. It is just as it is to be. Trust. We are here, even when it appears that we may not be. Do not doubt. Doubt will get you nowhere. But if doubt is all that there is in your heart, at this or any moment, then go ahead and doubt with all your heart, for this is what is to be for this moment. Accept that you doubt. Accept all that comes to you, for it is just as it is to be.

Do not worry about what should happen; take what comes and be thankful. Have no expectations and no fear. Take what comes along and bless it, for it is just as it was meant to be. There are no mistakes; there are no accidents; all is just as it should be. When you understand this, you will be at peace. Each event has a purpose under Heaven. Do not wish for things to be different in a moment of pain. Experience and move through the pain, and it will help you grow.

Embrace each moment, for each has a purpose and that purpose is to love, to learn, and to bring you closer to God. The same goes for every soul who is a person on earth; each has a purpose. No matter how lowly a person appears to be, he is there for a purpose. Embrace that person, for he is Love and he is learning. Do not condemn, for it is his journey. Embrace all circumstances as your own. They are your way to us. Know this and be still.

We have come to tell you that we love each soul for who it is. Whether it appears to be good or bad, all souls are good. They cannot help but be good. It is what they are. When you know that you are goodness, then you shall know us. For to know us, you must know your Self. Know your Self as goodness, and you will know yourself as "Godness." They are one and the same. You are good, and so you are God. You need not try to be good or God; just know that you are.

Your heart knows the way, for your heart is your soul, and your soul has always known the way. It has just been waiting for you to realize that it does. Know that your soul knows All, and you will know All. You have all the answers inside your soul. This is as it is to be. Follow your soul, and you will know All. We will help you to find your soul and we will help you to know All, but know that you already do know. Trust that you know All. Trust yourself, and you will remember.

December 30

We are here. This you must know. This you must believe. You come to hear all that we have to say and to learn your lessons. Take them into your heart, and then give them to another's heart. This is the way the message is to be passed on. Pass it on until everyone who wishes to know All knows. The message is for everyone who is ready to learn and ready to know. You are one of those who is ready. You are ready to hear our message of Love.

Our message is all about just that—Love. Love is the

answer to all questions. It will always take you to the highest part of your soul. Love all who come into your sight and your knowing, and you will do no harm. Love is the way to go, the place to be, and the way to All. Love all—beginning with yourself. Love yourself, and you will then be able to love all others. In your world you think that to love yourself is wrong, that it is conceit of some sort. Loving yourself and knowing that you are grand is not conceit; it is Love—Love of the highest kind. Loving yourself is the only way to loving another. Without having Love and the highest regard for yourself, you cannot have Love or regard for another.

You must do unto yourself before you can do unto another. For if you give to another what you have not given to yourself, you will experience jealousy. You will be jealous, for they have what you do not. Wars have been fought over this principle. This is the cause of all strife and arguments. When one has what the other does not, one will always feel slighted. Now imagine that you give all your love to others and forget to love yourself—this will cause a war within yourself, for you will become angry that you do not have what you have given away.

We expect others to give to us what we give freely to them, but it does not always work this way. You must be willing to give without expecting to receive. It is in the expectation of what you will get back that resentment will begin. You will resent, for you have given all of yourself, and you are not receiving from those you have given to. Resentment and jealousy—love is far away from these two principles. Love yourself, give to yourself, and then you will be able to love and to give to others without resentment. You will already have what you are giving away, and so you will not need to expect to be given it in return. You will know that you already have it.

Know you have the love for yourself and you are grand, and then give your love and grandness to others so that they may know just how grand they are. This is the way to pure Love, total Love, and Love for all without exception. We have come to you in this spirit of Love. We love ourselves, and so we can give all our Love to you. We are not expecting love in return, but should you love us, we will be so grateful. For when you can love us, then we will know that you already love yourself. This is as it is to be: love yourself above all others.

As the new year approaches, enter the world with a smile. Give your smile away to everyone. They are infectious! When you smile and others see it, they will smile. Smiles are God's way of coming to you on earth. Each time you smile, God is there pulling up the corners of your mouth. He is with you. Smile and know this.

There are so many sad ones—ones who have lost their ability to smile. This has happened, for they have forgotten that God is there waiting to tug at the corners of their mouth. Help them find their smiles. When someone does not smile at you, smile at them anyway. Do not worry that they will think you are out of your mind. Smile and know that you have done a good thing. The world needs your smile. Do not hide it. For if you hide it from the world, you are hiding it from God. God needs your smile; the world needs your smile. Smile and show God that you know He is with you. You will also get fewer wrinkles by smiling than by frowning. Yes, it's true. God does have a sense of humor. God laughs when you laugh and He smiles when you smile.

God will always be with you—through your smiles and your laughter and your tears. You will never be alone. When you smile, remember that God's Love is right there, right there in the corners of your mouth. Smile for yourself and for the world. Smile for God!

December 31

This is a day of great joy. It is the end of the days of pain. The world is coming to the New Dawn. All nations have come together in celebration of the New Millennium. Now all must come together in the celebration of Life. If you can come together for one day, why not every day? This is the question that you must ask yourselves: why not every day?

Each day can be a celebration of Love. All countries were joined today in the same cause, celebrating the New Millennium. Take this message and become One in all causes: the cause of peace, the cause of feeding the hungry, the cause of clothing and sheltering the homeless, and the cause of curing all ills. Work together on these causes. Forget all the fireworks and pageantry. Come together on all that is important. This you must learn. For until you learn this lesson, the world will be separate.

To become One, you must act and think as One. You must come together and be All to each other. None should have more than others, and none should have less. Share the wealth, and all will have what they need to live. These are the questions that you must answer. Can you become One? Can you accept each culture? Can you not judge it as right or wrong, but accept it for what it is? Can you accept all people for who they are—right now, the way they are—different from you? Can you become One with someone who is different than you? Can you become One with someone who has harmed you? This is the way to Oneness: see no differences, see all the same, and see all as One. You must learn this in order for the world to become united.

Lend a hand, help others, love others, and serve others. When you serve others, you serve your Self. The way to your Self is through the service of love. Give your love to others through service, and you shall know the love of your Self. This is the grandest Love that there is.

Enter the New Millennium with Love in your heart. Let the fireworks light up your life with Love. Let the celebration begin and never end. Celebrate the Life that God has given to you. Celebrate your soul. This is a new beginning for you. All has been wiped clean. You are pure. You are new. You may be whoever you wish to be.

This you must know: create who you are, and all will be just as you envision it. Envision it and make it real. Live your life as a celebration of the Love of God.

January 3

We come to tell you that we love you. You have been looking for us, and now you have found us. My name is Char, and I am the Goddess of Love. All the Love that you feel has originated in my heart. I am Pure Love, and now so are you. You have taken the Love out of the energy that surrounds your world and absorbed it into your heart. We can see that your heart is softening and growing. Your Love is now more than it was. This is as it is to be.

You are Love—Pure Love. In the New Millennium, let Love abound through all the lands. This is the Age of Aquarius. Aquarius is Love—Love for all mankind, Love for all creatures, and Love for you. Love has come to your world. Take this Love and use it wisely. Use it only for the good of all. Use it to promote the healing of all your land's scars. There are so many wounds to heal, but Love will heal them all. Know this and you will heal. Love is the way to strength and to courage. When you have Love, you have All.

Love is like a shining prism. Just as each color radiates through the prism, all things radiate through Love. Just as a prism is clear, all is clear through Love. Love clears all the negativity from the heart and replaces it with Love. See Love in all things, and your heart will be a clear prism of Love. It will shine in all things, to all people, at all times. It will not stop to take the time to question whether this situation deserves Love. It will give it automatically. This is the way of the heart that is pure.

It will come to you. Know this: it will come. Do not be impatient waiting for purity. You cannot wait for it, for if you do, it shall never come. For if you wait, you are expecting, and expectation will bring nothing. Do not wait; just know that your heart is a prism. See your heart reflecting Love to all. When you just know that it is, it will be. This is all it takes: no work, no wishing, and no hoping—just know.

Be who you are—a Prism of Pure Love. Love is all there is. It is all that there has ever been. When you understand this and take it into your heart, then you will know All. You will be one of us. You will be a Goddess of Love, just as I am. Do not wait. Just be what you truly are—a Prism of Pure Love.

January 5

This you must know: we will keep you safe from all harm. You need not fear when you are with us, and you are always with us. No harm can come to you when you are in the arms of God. All has been planned just as you created it. Do not worry, for everything has a reason. This you must know and trust.

You have come here to find All—all about the mysteries of your world and ours. Be still as we tell you about them. Do not fear for what is to be said, for it will all be said in Love. We need not keep you safe from yourself. Your soul will create only what it needs to learn so that it may find its way to us. Know this and be still.

Do not fear, for if you fear life you shall never live it. Take it in, embrace each and every moment, and you will have a life lived well. Live your life in the Now. Be in the moment fully, and you shall know the delightfulness of your life and all it has to offer.

We have come to tell you about the Love and the Light. Both are within your reach, for they are within you. Both are given to you by the Universal Spirit that is God. Both are flames that burn brightly within your soul. They are there. Know that they are there.

January 6

This you must know: we will come to you whenever you wish us to be with you. All you need to do is ask. Ask with sincerity, and we will come to you. Each of you has the ability to hear us. Each can do it. You must desire it and create it. Do not want it, for if you want, you will only experience wanting. Desire and create.

You do not realize your own power. You can do or be anything that you desire. You are the grandest creation of God; now be the grandest creator. Know that you are co-creating your world with God. You have been created—now create. This is as it was meant to be. It is not blasphemy. It makes God smile to know that you understand that you and He are One. This you must know: God is with you each and every moment. He will never leave you alone. This you must know: there will always be two sets of footprints in the sand. And if you see only one set, it is then that you were being carried by the Lord.

You have come to us for the gift of learning. Take all that we say, place it in your heart, and make it yours. Only when you make it yours will you be able to learn. Take all the knowledge that is rightfully yours and place it into your heart, but do not let it sit there alone and in the dark. Use your Light to tell all who wish to know. Give them the gift of learning. Help them to find their Light so that they may help others. Know that you, too, can be a messenger for God. Pass these lessons on to others so that they may learn and know. Help all others co-create their realm. Imagine what a wonderful place earth could be if everyone were creating the perfect world. Imagine how the earth would glow with Love. The time is coming. You must know: it will happen. It is always darkest before the dawn. Know this and be still.

Do not fear what people will think of you. Put your understanding out there and let all who wish to learn grab on and take the knowledge. And for those who are not ready yet, do not judge their skepticism. Do not judge their laughter, for it is in the laughter that they will begin to think. They will begin to think, *perhaps, this is true.* They shall see how happy you are, and they will wonder. It is in this wonder they will realize that they are ready. Know this and you will understand the power that lies in your heart.

You can use your power to create your world. Go out into the world with your smile and create. Create others who understand your message. Create the world as it should be. Know this: you have power. You have all the power of God and of the Heavenly Realm. This you must know: you have our power.

Believe and all will be grand. You will know just how grand you really are, and just how grand your earth could be. Summon up your courage to believe it is there. All the courage you need is in your heart, as well as all the Love, the Light, and the Knowing. Just know it is there, and you will know All.

January 7

We are Love and you are Love. We have come to tell you the great story of Love; the story of Jesus Christ; the story of God. He was Love to all. He believed that all could be done, and He knew that He had it inside Him. He did not question whether or not it was there; He just knew. You must know, too. You must believe and trust that it is there.

When you believe, all things are possible. Life will never be the same when you believe. Believe in God and believe in the power of your Self. You are the true Spirit of God come to earth to live out all things. When you come to know this, you will know All. It is right there within you. Believe that you are God, and you will be. Believe that you know All, and you will. Do not doubt that All will happen. Keep the faith burning brightly in your heart. As moments of doubt creep in, look at them fully, honor them for what they are, and then let them go. They are not worthy of your time. Trust in God, for He trusts in you.

January 8

The journey has only begun. Do not worry about how long the journey will take; just know that every day is as it was meant to be. You are only beginning to scratch the surface. This will be the journey of a lifetime. Do not worry about arriving. It will happen when it is time. Do not fear, for you will not arrive before it is time. You have much to learn, and this is only the beginning. You will be with us for a lifetime of lifetimes. It does not end. Do not forget that it does not end.

When your mortal life is over, you will still be alive. Do not lose sight of this teaching; it is the most important one. You will be alive. Even as your body is put into the ground, your soul will be alive. The essence of you—of who you are—will be alive. Only the container will perish, and there is always another container. Do not fear, for there is no end. This you must know. This you must understand: you—who you truly are—will live forever. Know this and do not fear.

All is just as it is meant to be. You have come to us in Love, and Love is all that you need to know. Put the fear and the anger and the pettiness away. You do not need them anymore; but if you do, then take them out and use them. We do not judge. Each is perfect in its own moment. Fear when you need to fear. If who you are is pettiness, then be it. Be it with all your heart, and know that we are not judging that you have chosen to be petty.

If where you wish to be is jealous and angry, then go there with all your heart. It is the only way you will learn that jealousy and anger are not who you are. You must learn who you are not before you can know who you are. Know this and accept it, for it is in the learning of who you are not that you will learn who you are. You are still learning. Do not judge yourself. This is a journey. Do not expect to arrive immediately.

Do you expect your newborn to get up and walk within days or weeks? No, and so do not expect that you shall know All within days or weeks. You are a newborn. You are learning. Do not place time restraints on what you feel you need to know. It will all happen exactly when it is meant to happen. Let all just "be." Let your Self just "be." All is perfect right now. You have already come so far in your journey toward Home. You do not know who your soul started out to be so many lifetimes ago. Savor the moments and do not wish to be here immediately. We will enjoy the journey with you, helping you along the way. Know this and be still. You will never be alone. No matter how many lifetimes it takes for you to come Home—we will be there. Be still and know that we will be there.

150

Call us into your heart, and we will be there. Call us into your life, and we will be there in a flash. When you feel helpless, call to us and we will be at your side cradling you like a child. When you are angry, call us and we will be there placing all our Love within your heart so that you may glow only with Love. When you are hurt, call us and ask us to help you understand what has happened.

You are beginning to understand, but there is so much more to learn. Do not try to learn it all at once. Be happy where you are, for you are at the perfect place, at the perfect moment. See all for the perfection that it is. See all your anger and hurt and pettiness for the perfection that it is. It is in this perfection that you will learn just who you are. Know this and be still. And when you have finished learning one lesson, you will move on, for there will always be more lessons to learn.

Take notice, be aware, and your heart will change. And as your heart changes, so will your mind, for it knows who is really in charge. Your soul will take over as lessons are learned. This you must know: be patient with yourself. Be loving with yourself. This you must believe: you are perfect.

January 10

You must follow your intuition—that Voice that tells you about your soul. Your intuition is your internal guide, and it will always lead you to the highest experience. Take the leap of faith and follow. Follow your innermost desires, and you will find your highest desire. It is calling you. It has always been calling you. Have no fear—listen. Your soul will take you to the heights of exaltation, for it knows All. Follow your soul's desire, for it will take you to the All-in-All.

Forget what the mind thinks it wants. It does not know. It is influenced by the world, by friends, and by commercials. It thinks that it needs things like clothes, cars, and objects to prove it is a success. The soul needs none of these things to understand that it is a success. It knows that just by "being" it is successful. For to the soul, success is learning the lessons which will bring it to its highest experience.

Your soul will speak to you, and when you listen, it will speak more often and more clearly. Know that God and your Self will lead you only where you want to go. Your soul will speak volumes as to what you want, but it is up to you to listen. It has always been speaking. It does know the Way. This you must know: it knows the Way.

Trust the notion to call a friend or take a different route home. Those inside voices are there to lead you. Listen to them, for when you listen to the voices, you will know the Way. Your soul contains all our voices. Your soul has taken all our wisdom and gently gives it to you when you are ready. The more you listen and follow, the more your soul will know that you are ready, and the more it will let us speak to you.

Do not think that we have not been with you all the days of your life. We have been there—speaking to you. Know this and be comforted. You have never been alone. This is how it has always been and this is how it will always be. You shall never be alone. We will always be right there within your soul, waiting for you to listen.

Listening is the Way. Follow and you shall find All. God is waiting. You are the Light. You are Love. You are the Way.

January 11

This you must know: you are the co-creator with God. You have come together with all the souls of the Universe to create your world. This world is of your own doing.

Once you realize and believe this, you will be able to create consciously. You will be One with all the creators. You will be God.

When all in the world understand this, you will be able to live in a world of peace and harmony. All will create exactly what they need—no more and no less. This is as it is meant to be. All having—none wanting. For if all the "haves" take only what is necessary, there will be plenty for those who need. This is a concept that you as humans do not understand.

You have not realized that what you do to another you have done to yourself. When you condemn another, you condemn yourself. When you judge another, you judge yourself. When you love another, you have shown love to yourself. This is how it works. This is how it has always worked.

Your world will be glorious and shine with all the Love of the Universe when all know this one thing: you are all One. You are not separate. You are One. Do not believe all those predictions of doom and destruction. Your world will be saved, and it will be glorious. You are at the dawning of a new beginning. More of your inhabitants are learning the lessons of the soul. They will learn, and as they pass them on to others, the energy of their learning will become One with the energy of others. It will grow, taking in more and more souls. And the souls will be happy because they have been waiting for this.

You can do much, even though you are only one. One is the biggest thing that you can be. When you are only One, you are All. One is the best thing that you could be, so do not fear that you are only one person and can accomplish nothing on your own. Become One and you will know the Way.

January 12

All is perfect and all is Divine. You are the Divine Creation of God, as He is your Divine creation. It is one continuous circle. You are Him and He is you. You have been created by Him, just as He has been created by you. Without Him creating you, you could not be, and without you creating Him, He could not be. It is a circle—a Circle of Love. This is how it has always been.

Your life shall never end. It, too, is one continuous circle. The love that you send to others is the love that is given back to you. This—a circle as well. What you do for others, you have done for Me, and you have done for your Self. A circle—always a circle. This is how it has been planned. This is how it will always be.

There are breaks in the circle on earth. People have forgotten. They have known, but they have forgotten. It is time to remember. It is time to close the circle. For when everyone remembers, the earth shall be a continuous circle again, and it will be grand. One creating the other, one honoring the other, one cherishing the other, and one loving the other—a complete Circle of Love.

You are beginning to remember. You have come to learn, and learn you shall. I shall teach you things that are grand. Never fear that I am not with you. I am near always. We are a circle. This you must remember: we are a Circle of Love. Do not let past teachings get in the way of remembering. It is time to put all false teachings of Me behind you. Know this: I am pure, just as you are pure. Put all in the past, and I will teach you now. I will teach you of all the Love that I have for you. You are my precious child, and I will protect you always. Come to Me to learn. Leave the teachings of others behind. It is time to remember.

Remember, and you will find your way Home. I am the Way. You are the Way. One continuous circle. Follow Me and you will remember. All is within your soul already; you must just remember. Remember this: I will love you unconditionally—forever. There is nothing you can do that will make Me not love you. You are Mine. I will love you forever—and forever is forever. No conditions. No expectations. No doubts. Forever. This is how it is to be.

You do not have to worry about making mistakes that will offend Me. There is nothing that you can do to offend Me. All is just as it is meant to be. Know this and be still. You have come to Me to learn, and I will be the Great Teacher. And when you have learned your lessons, then you, too, shall go forth into the world and send My message to all who wish to know. You have been given these messages for a reason, and that reason is to pass them on. Then you will have become the Great Teacher.

Remember: no expectation and no fear. Do not let the human side of you worry about My expectations; I have none. Take this to heart and remember that I will love you forever.

January 13

We are Love and you are Love. These words are meant to be passed on to all who will listen. These words are for each who has come to this book to learn. They are for each soul who is ready to know who it really is. The words are given to you as a comfort. They are meant to give you Hope, to give you Peace, and to give you Love—all of which you will then pass on to the world.

You have come here for a reason; it did not just happen. You created it. You were ready to know All, and so you are here. This is how it is and this is how it will always be. The soul knows when you are ready and it rejoices, for it has always been ready. We have come to you so that you may learn all that your soul wants to learn. This is a time of

155

great joy. Know joy and you will know God. Know joy and you will know your Self.

The words which are written here are given to you by the Angelic Realm in the spirit of hope—hope that you will let your soul learn. You must step away from the normalcy of life and let go. Let go and let God. This has been said many times, but few are able to truly do this. Do not worry. Just let go. All will be taken care of. All is perfect, exactly as it is.

This you must know: Love is all there is. All else is just an illusion, and the illusions of your world are great. So many live in the illusion that it can be hard to see past it, but you can do it. See past all that is not Love, and you will see right through the illusion. The fog will lift, and all you will see is Love. We are within all the Love that is not illusion. Love on your earth can be an illusion, so watch carefully. Our Love is pure Love, and pure Love will conquer all illusion.

Earth lives in the illusion of time. Time is really not happening. It is all happening right now. All your life now and all your lives before are all happening now. It is called the Eternal Now. It goes on forever, placing each moment exactly where it should be: Now. You must live for the Now, for this is where All is. All is in the Eternal Now. All the Happiness, all the Joy, and all the Love is now. Right now—in the Eternal Now.

Live All right now. Do not wait for times to be perfect, for the perfect time is now. You will come to understand this as you begin to know who you really are. For who you really are is Love and Joy and Happiness.

Enter the Eternal Now. We have been waiting. This is your chance to know All. Pick up your mat and follow us. Open your eyes, and you will see. Let all the illusion fade away like the morning mist, and you will see it, for it is right there. The Eternal Now can be yours.

January 14

We are here. We are glad that you are here, too. We look forward to having you come to us to learn. We know you look forward to having us come to tell you about the wonders of our world. This is a story of Love. Your life will become this story, but it will take time for your earthly life to understand all that is happening to it.

You are beginning to understand that this is a lifetime change. Lifetime changes can be frightening. Do not be frightened. You are ready for this change. You have prepared for a lifetime of lifetimes to come to where you are right now. When you live the changes and take them into your heart, they can cause confusion within the body. Be with the confusion. It is part of the journey.

Do not worry about where others are on the path. This is not a race. We do not compete. All will win in their own time. Do not compare your journey with others on the path if it means that you are competing to see who is the farthest. There is no way to know who is ahead. Each is on his own path, and no two paths are the same. There is no way to judge who is closer to Home.

Do not judge, for when you judge you place doubts in your heart as to whether the trip is worthy of your effort. Do not place any doubt. This is your trip—no one else's. Do not compare, do not compete, and do not judge. These are earthly terms, and they do not apply to your journey. You will be where you need to be at exactly the time you need to be there. This you must know: your journey is perfect. Do not think of it as anything else. It is where it is meant to be. And when you arrive, everyone will be there. For everyone will arrive at exactly the same moment—the moment of the Eternal Now. No one will finish first and no one will finish last. It is all perfect just as it is. Know this and be still.

Let go of your earthly desire to compete. There is no need for it. For if you win, you are ecstatic; but if you lose, you are sad. There can only be one winner, and the ecstasy fades quickly. When you come to us, you will always be a winner; you will always be ecstatic; and you will always be first. Do not waste your energy competing on earth. Know that you are a winner in God's eyes, and become that winner in your own eyes. You are perfect—just as you are.

Know this and you will know Peace—the Peace of the Love of God. Know this Peace, and you will truly know your Self. You have already won. No need to wait for the partying. Party now, for you have already won the race!

January 15

You are the grandest of God's creations, for you have created yourself. We love you, for it is within you that we are born. It is within your own creation that we are given life. We lie quiet in the non-existence until someone creates us in his mind. And then we fly. We have been waiting to fly with you, and now is the time. You have created us, and now we have life in your realm. Come fly with us. Know that you are an angelic soul, too, and come fly with us.

You have chosen and created human life in order to experience who you really are, but know that you are one of us also. You are an angelic voice in our Realm. You can be everywhere at any time. You are not confined to only your human container; you can be All at the same time. You are with us right now, and it is glorious. Here with us you are smiling, for now your human life knows this also. Know this and be this.

You can be here and you can be there all at the same time, for time does not exist except on earth. All is forever—right now—at this moment. Time is a bubble in which All is happening. The bubble twists and changes shape as it dances alongside the sun in the gentle spring breeze. This is time; it twists and turns and changes shape, but never is it not everything. All is enclosed in that bubble of time. All is enclosed with the rememberings of your life. You know All. All has always been there. All will never leave. You know All, for All is right within your soul. Remember. It will take no work. It will take no studying. It will just happen. When you fill your life with all that is Love, your soul will remember. It will remember the gloriousness of being with us, and it will fly. It is happening right now within your bubble of time.

Be with us in Spirit, and you will be with us always. We are always with you because you are always with us. You can never *not* be with us for we are you. Come fly with us. Remember that you can fly, and you will, for All is within you already. Do not doubt that it is there; it is. All is within your reach. Remember and it will be there. You have all the answers you will ever need within your own soul. Remember, and come to us. We are waiting to fly with you.

January 17

You have come in Love and in Light. Listen to our words. They are grand. Do not worry that you will not hear them. Listen, for they are there. You can all hear the songs of our hearts. We are with each of you. This you must know. This you must believe: we love you with all our hearts. Our Love for you is as wide as the ocean and as deep as the Universe. We will love you always. Love is all there is—today and tomorrow.

There is no need to fear that life will not turn out as you planned. Each event is a chance to learn and to grow. Look at each event—no matter how painful—as the gift that it is meant to be. Thank God for each gift. These events help you remember who you are. This is how it works: you already know, and now you must just remember. If you believe, life will bring all that you wish. Believe that you are the creator of all you see. Believe and you can create the world for the highest good of all. You must know this: you are God. Create. It is your destiny. Awaken to the Spirit that is within you. It is calling to get out. It knows who you are, and it needs to tell you. The Spirit is calling for you to know All.

Follow your Spirit's call. It shall lead you Home. It knows the way. Follow the music in your soul, for it knows the way. Follow the Love which radiates from your being. Your being knows the way Home. It knows the way. We are within your heart and your soul and your being. We know the way Home. You know the way Home. Trust your heart and your soul and your being.

There is no need to fear, for all is well. You will not be alone. There are many on this journey. You may feel that you are the only one, but fear not. You are not alone; there are many—all on their way Home. Follow your very being where it wants to go, for it knows the way.

January 18

This is our story of Love. Love is all there is. It is the only thing there is. You must know this. You must believe this. This is the meaning of Life. Without Love, there is nothing. To know All is to love all. All will love when All has been placed at the head of their lives. Love is All. This is our story. This is our song. It is being given to you as a gift so that you may know All, so that you many remember and give All to all.

We have come to tell you about the secrets of life. The biggest secret is life does not end. Take this teaching and make it your own. Own it to the very core of your being. There is no need to fear the death of life. When a loved one has passed over to his new lifetime, do not grieve. Rejoice, for the soul has learned and is ready to move on. There is no end to life. Rejoice for the time the soul has had on earth. Do not be sad, for as the body dies the soul is reborn. It meets the All-in-All which is God, and knows All. It bursts with Love and Joy and bounces all over. It is so happy, for it has been freed, and it can fly.

Do not be sad as the shadow of death takes over the eyes of your loved ones. It is a time to rejoice. When you know that life does not end, you will know that you have no need to be sad. Others will not understand, but they will see the peace in your heart. As you say goodbye to your dearly departed, they will question why you are not in complete mourning. They will wonder, but they will wish for the peace that they can see in your eyes. Give them your peace, and it will grow so that they may understand.

Mourn the loss of your loved one's earthly form, but do not mourn the loss of their Spirit. It will always be there, and if you are willing to listen, it will come to you and speak of all the joys it has found. It is a time of celebration. Each physical death is a chance to choose the next life. It could be a life lived on earth; a life lived to learn more lessons. Look for your loved one. It may take many lifetimes, but there are those who cross our paths whom we know we have known before. It is a feeling—an inkling—and so often you push it aside as nonsense. It is not. It is your intuition telling you that you know this soul.

Honor this feeling. It is you remembering, and remembering is the way Home. It is not New Age who-ha. It is the Way. All who do not believe will make fun and call it witchcraft or nonsense, but those who know will not pay mind to the nonbelievers. They will not judge those who do not believe.

Do not dismiss things that you do not see as possible. All is possible in the realm of your creation. Create and it is possible. Cure a disease. Bring a loved one to you. Get the job. Find a mate. It is possible. Just create, but create without expectations. For it is in the expectations that you will see failure. For when you expect a result, and it does not happen, then you will be disappointed. It is in the disappointment that the seeds of disbelief are planted. Create and know that whatever happens is exactly what you have created, and it has been created for a reason.

Know that you create not only consciously, but also subconsciously. So what you do not think that you have created has been created by you. Know that nothing in your life has not been created by your soul. Your soul is in charge of your destiny. Begin to create consciously, and you will eventually be able to create subconsciously in a deliberate way. Right now your subconscious creates what you need out of what you fear and what you hope. They are mere thoughts in the back of your mind, and they are there through the years of your life. These are ideas which your conscious mind has forgotten, but they are still there. They could be positive or they could be negative ideas, or they could be ideas of fear or ideas of a grand life that you just could not believe. Know that they are there.

It is when you can create with these subconscious ideas that the joy will be lifted from the past. For when you can take the negative and fearful thoughts from the subconscious, look at them and honor them for what they are, it is then that you can take them from the subconscious and give them away to the wind. Let the breezes blow them far from your life, for you will know that you no longer need them. But when you take all the things that you thought were not possible and look at them fully, you will know that they are possible. You will know that all you have to do is believe, see, and create. Look at them fully, take them into your heart, and make them a part of your life.   When you learn to create consciously, your subconscious will begin calling, for it will know that you can create. Begin to create. Know that it is, and it will be, but do not be disappointed if what is created appears not to be your doing. It is. It will always be.

Honor the negative and fearful events. It is your subconscious taking them out and looking at them so that it may let them go. Do not hang on to that which you know your soul wants to give to the wind. Do not struggle with your soul. Know that it knows, and you will know All. Honor each and every event in your life as a gift from God and as a gift from your Self, for that is what it is—a gift from yourself so that you may know your Self. Know this and be still.

We have come to tell you this so that you may look at your life in a new light—the Light of Love—the Light of God. It is within God's Light that you will see that All is possible. It is within your Light that you will know the meaning of your life. Know that the Light is there, and you will know All. Remember it is there. All you have to do is to know that you know.

Life is a learning process. It is the growing up of your soul. Honor that child, honor that old soul, honor who you are exactly where you are. It is in the acceptance of who you are now, that you will find who you really are.

January 19

We have come to you to tell of the Love we have for your earth. We love you and wish that you would come to the Light. Our Light is bright. If you look, you will see the glow of the Love in our hearts. The glow becomes brighter each time a human believes what is in his soul and comes to the Light.

When you come to the Light, you will know the Love of the Heavens. It is always within you. Until you have come and seen the Light, you will not be aware of the Love. Yes, it can be like the light bulb going on above your head.

It can be that dramatic at the moment you "get it" or it can be a gradual coming to know that it is there. Do not judge how the Light comes to you. Know that it is there, and it will come in whatever fashion that need be. The Light is within you. It has always been there. This is Char. I am teaching you today. You have come to me to know all about the Love and Light and the Eternal Now.

These are the things that you need to know: you are Love, you are Light, and you live in the Eternal Now. All else is not as important as these three things. Follow these Truths, and all else will follow and come to you. You are Love. You are Light. You live in the Eternal Now. Clutch these Truths to your breast, and hold them tightly until they have penetrated your chest and entered your heart. Your soul knows these as Truths. Let your heart know also.

Believe that you are Love. Believe that you are Light. Believe that you live in the Eternal Now, and it will be so. Create it. It is that simple. You have all the skill that you need. Your soul knows the way. Believe that it does.

January 21

This is how your life shall be. It shall be a Complete Circle of Love. It is there; all you have to do is live it. Do not want it or think about it or question it, just live it. When you live it, you will be it. You will be the Complete Circle of Love.

Do not fear that you are not there now. Knowing is being aware. You are aware when you are not being Love. To know what Love is not is the first step. Be kind to yourself when you are not Unconditional Love. Give yourself time to learn. It will not happen all at once. Anything worthwhile is worth waiting and working for. You will come to be Unconditional Love when you are completely aware—aware of what Unconditional Love is, and aware of what it is not. When you know the difference, you will be able to be what you are. You will be a part of the Divine Circle of Love.

The Divine Circle of Love will bring you Home. It will bring you to All. All is within this Circle. You have been on the outside, for you knew no differently. You were not aware. You were sleeping. You did not know it was there. Now that you do, you will not be able to ignore it. You will want to get it. This is the way: knock and the door shall open. Ask and you shall receive. Create and you shall be. Create a Circle of Unconditional Love, and you shall find that you are in the middle of it.

Love is the beginning and the end, the Alpha and the Omega. God is the beginning and the end, the Alpha and the Omega. You are the beginning and the end. You are the Alpha and the Omega. You are Love and you are God. Know this and be still.

January 24

You are Love and you are Light. Do not forget these things. You are Love because Spirit can be nothing but Love. You are Light because the soul sends out the goodness of your spirit and it shines, for you are God.

We have come to tell you all that you need to know. You have listened so patiently, but there is more, so much more; for when you have learned All, there will always be more. Do not fear that when you know All, we will come with the hands of God and strike you down. You will not reach the All-in-All until your soul knows it is time. And then in a burst, you will be with God; you will be part of the All-in-All. Knowing us will enrich and increase your life, not shorten it. Do not fear knowing. Knowing is grand.

We have come to tell you that we love you. Love is all there is. Know this. Things will begin to become clear when you see your life and all others through Love. All will become clear as crystal, for you will know their hearts. You will see their insides and their outsides, and you will know them well. Heal the dark spots within their souls, and their wounds will heal. Love is all there is. Know this and be Love.

You are the beginning of a new time on earth. It shall happen. Do not be impatient. Know that others are following your Light. They are following, and you are not even aware that they are. Watch for the changes in the souls around you. See your family change little by little. It will happen—not all at once, but it will happen. They will feel your love, and they will know that it is safe to be who they are. They will not feel the sting of criticism; they will feel the Love. They will not feel the hurt of condemnation, they will feel the Love. They will not feel the coldness of judgment, they will feel the Love. This will make even the hardest heart change.

When your family and all others know that they are safe to be who they are without criticism, condemnation, or judgment, they will be grand. Believe this can happen, and it shall be so. Create it and it will be. Create a home filled with Love. Do not judge them when they fight or argue. Let them be. The only way for them to find out who they are is by finding out who they are not. This is the way. It is the way for each of us. It was your way. Know this and be patient. When all know that they are safe within your love, the miracles shall begin to happen. Suddenly, as if overnight, they will become softer and more loving. Be patient and you shall see this, but do not expect, for nothing can come of expectation. Know. Know that all will be peaceful within your life, and it will be.

The key is to know—not to hope—but to know. When you create hope, you have not created the happening. But when you know, then it has already happened. There is no hoping or waiting, for you know that it has already arrived.

166

Know that you already have, and you will. It may seem hard in the beginning to convince your human self that you have what it perceives that it does not, but be gentle. Know and your human self will follow, for your soul is stronger. Your human self wants to believe; it just needs a little more time to be convinced. It has witnessed all the hardships and all the unanswered wishes, and so it is skeptical. Be patient. Just know that your human self will come to be with your soul, and it will, for it has already happened. Know and it has already happened.

Know that there is peace in the world, and there will be peace. Do not give up, for this will not happen overnight. The reality is that there is peace on earth. You just do not know it yet. You hope for it, but in the hoping you do not accept that it has already happened. Know that it is so, and it will be. Know that all the people on earth are good, and they will be. Know that you are God, and you will be. It is as simple as this. It is so simple that many will not believe. Know that you are happy, and you will be. And when all around you see your happiness, it will make them happy also. Know that you have enough material things, and you will have enough. For it is in the wanting, you feel that you do not have. Know that you have enough of what you need, and you will have it.

See how simple it is. Do not try. Just "be." Just be All, and you will know All. Just know that you know All, and you will be All. One continuous circle. The Divine Circle of Life. Know and be. Be the Divine Circle of Love. Know and be.

January 25

This you must know: Love is a many splendored thing. There are many splendors when you love. Know this and be Love. Char is the Goddess of Love, and she has come to you. She will be with you always to help you recognize Love. Know that you are Love—all Love. This is the way to become Love: just know that you are Love.

Jeremy will bring you peace. He is the Angel of Peaceful Times. Keep him in your heart, and you will know the peace that is God. Know that there is nothing but peace, and this is what you will see. Peace is all around you. Know that it is there and it will be.

Sam knows you. He is the Keeper of the Heart. Your heart will be safe when Sam is here. He will calm the hurt so that you may see the lessons. He will help you understand the ways of the heart.

Daniel is a Guardian Angel. He may not be your guardian angel, but you can know yours. You may know your guardian angel by asking the Heavens for his or her name. Ask in the quiet of the night, and you shall hear the name whispered in your ear. If you do not hear at first, ask again. They will be glad to tell you a little louder. Know that the name of your guardian angel is there in the still of the night, and you will hear it when you ask.

Da will bring you soothing music. He will light up your life with the songs of the Angelic Realm. Listen for them. You shall hear them at times of great joy and at times of despair. When you hear the ringing in your ears, know that it is Da's soothing music. The noise is not noise at all, but music. It shall come at times when you need to know that we are here.

Watch and you will be amazed. We will be there. These are some of the Angelic Realm. Look to us at times when you need guidance. We will always be there. We are waiting for you to know us. Come to us, and we will celebrate the joys of Life—of Eternal Life, of a Life that never ends, of a Life that is All.

January 27

We have come to tell you of the love we have for you. It is grand. You are Love and we are Love. This you must know: we love you. My name is George, and I am the Keeper of the Light which is within your heart. Know me and you will know the Light.

My Light is strong—strong enough for all to see—strong enough for you to know that I am there. Let your Light shine through my Light, and it will be doubled in strength. Our Light will shine together so all may know. This you must know: you are not alone. Your Light will never be one; it will always be many. You will always have our Light shining with yours.

Your Light will bring strength to all. You can be a Guiding Light to all who wish to know us. You can go out into the world and shine your Light so that all may see. Shining does not necessarily mean telling others of us. Shining your Light means being Love to all, seeing Love in all, and doing things that shine only Love. See Love in all people, in all situations, at all times. When you do this, you are shining God's Light. Do not expect perfection, for when you expect, it will not be there. Know that you are perfect. Know that your Light is perfect. Know that the time is perfect. See perfection in all you do, in all people, at all times. Do not judge perfection by your human terms. All is perfection.

Be Love. Seek Love. Act as Love would act. This shall be your mantra. Say it to yourself several times a day. Say it to yourself when you know there is a situation that needs Love. Remind yourself of the Light. Remind yourself of the Love. Be Love. Seek Love. Act as Love would act.

You are Love. This is the natural state of being. Being—not doing. Do not try to "do" love; just "be" Love. Just "be." You have come to us to know Love, and you have found it. Know that it is here, and that you have it. It will always be yours. It is yours to keep and yours to give away. For when you give your love away, it will come back twice as strong. And when you give your Light away, it too, will return twice as bright. Give so that all may have. Give so that you may receive more. Give your blessing, and you will receive a double portion of God's blessings.

You are Love. You are Light. You are heart. You are soul. Bring your Love, your Light, your heart, and your soul into alignment, and you will be All. You are on the path to knowing All. It is the path to us. It is the path to your Self. It is the path to God. Come, for we are waiting. We will take each step with you along the path. You will never walk alone. This is the way. Follow your heart. It is filled with Light.

January 29

This you must know: it is a time of great wonder. It is a time when all is becoming clear. Know that any pain you face now will bring clarity to your journey. Do not deny it. Your pain is a clearing of the soul. Do not regret that you are remembering. You are re-membering, which means that you are once again becoming a member with us. Re-membering. It is the way to us. You must remember to re-member and become whole. Embrace all your memories, painful and happy, for it is the way. Your soul is clearing so that you may have the room to learn more. You have come so far. Do not lose faith. It is your path.

You have become a messenger. You are showing your Light to others; you are knowing. Do you see the knowing? It is the Way. You are the Way. Our hearts are singing the praises of God—the God which is you. We are singing, for you are beginning to know.

170

You know. Now you must *know* you know. It is all there under the pain and the sorrow. All the knowing is there; all you must do is remember. You are a perfect creation. It is all within your soul. You have learned so many lessons, and now the time for beginning to know has come. Come to us, and you will know.

February 1

We have come in the spirit of Love and in the spirit of the Light. We know you have come in that same spirit. You are Light. You are Love. You are Spirit. We know.

Love is coming to your heart. We can tell. You are changing. You may not even see it yet, but we do. You are becoming the Spirit of the Light.

We need you to go out into the world and be that Light. Shine unto the world so that all may see and know. Know that you are Light. Know that it is in each and every one of you. Jesus was that Light, and now so are you. Do not be afraid to be a Light unto the world. You are for whom they have been waiting. You are the Messiah. Spread your Light and Love, and you will be the Messiah.

You will be our messenger of Love— nothing less and nothing more. Live Love, and you will be that Messenger. My eyes are swelling with tears of joy to know that you are Mine. I have been waiting for you, my child. And now you have come, just as I knew that you would. You have come to see the glory that is us. You have come to see the glory of a life lived with Me. I am always here. I always have been and I always will be. You are Mine and I am yours. Together we will conquer the world of darkness. Do not be afraid to enter the darkness. It can do you no harm. You are safe, for I am with you. This you must know: you will never be alone. You have come to Me and opened your heart, and now I will always be in your life because you know that I am there.

You cannot go back. Your life has changed, for you know Me. And you know that I know you. Personally. I know the innermost workings of your heart. These I have always known, but now you know that I know. This changes all things. Now that you know I know, you will become all that you were meant to be.

Together there is nothing that cannot be accomplished. We are One. You, Me, and all of us. We are One. Spread this word. Spread the New Gospel: we are One. Know this to the very core of your being. Know this to the very core of your soul. We are One. There is no difference. There is no separation. We are One.

What you do to others, you have done to Me and you have done to your Self. When you harm another, (which you cannot) you have actually harmed your Self (which you cannot.) There is no harm—only lessons. But in your life you know it as harm, and so when you harm another, you take that guilt into your heart. And when you take the guilt into your own heart, you have harmed yourself.

We are all good; none of you is bad. There is no bad or wrong. All are good; some just don't know it yet. Give them Love, and they will know that they are good. It is the ones who appear to be the worst souls that need the Love the most. They do not believe that they are good, so you need to convince them that they are. Show Love to all, and all will know that they are good. For when you show Love to all, you have shown Love to Me and to your Self. What you do for another, you have done for Me and you have done for your Self. Show Love to all, and you will know Love. Give to all, and all will be given to you. Be with another, and you will be with Me. See Me in the eyes of all. Do not look for Me so that you can treat Me differently. Do not look for Me so that you can honor and cherish Me. Do not look in your prayers for Me. Do not wait until you see the face of God to give goodness. See the face of God in all the world, for all in the world are God.

Show Love to all, and you will have shown Love to God. Show kindness, compassion, and Light to all in the world, and you will have shown it to God. For what you do for the least of the world, you have done for Me. For I am them and they are Me. This is what the passage in the Bible has always meant. No one has interpreted it quite this literally before. Most do not understand, but now you do. The world is God and God is the world.

Be with the people—all people of all color, religion, and diversity. Be with them, for they are Me. We are One. All of us. None is separate. All are One. Know this and you will know God. Know this and your world will light up with the Love. This is the way. You are the Way. I am the Way. They are the Way. All are the Way. Come to know and believe this.

Cherish each life as you cherish Mine, and you will be the Way. We come to tell you that you are the messenger; you are the Messiah. Do not be afraid. You have always been the Messiah. You are here to change the world. You are here to know and tell. Know, and tell all who will listen. Do not judge those who call you blasphemous, for they know not what they say. They will come when it is their time. It is your time now—right now. Do not let it pass. You have come too far. Your soul will not let you go back into the unknowingness. You cannot go back. You are here. You know Me. You know your Self.

Face the darkness, and you will be the victor. The darkness cannot hurt you, for you have the shield of God, and that shield will protect you. Even in death, you will be protected. It protected Jesus, even as he hanged dying on the cross. It protected him and gave him Eternal Life. You, too, will have Eternal Life. Do not fear when you die here on earth that it is the end. It is not. Never fear death. My shield will protect your Eternal Life, and you will become One with Me. Know this and go out into the world. Spread your Light, spread the Joy that is God, and spread the Love that is the Angelic Realm. All is real. Spread Love and Light and Joy to all in the world.

For what you do for the least of you, you have done for Me. Know this and be the messenger. Go out and be God. Yes, be God. Know that you are God and go out and be God. You are Me and I am you. We are One. No separation. I cannot say this enough times so that you shall know it in your heart. We are One. All are One. When you harm another, you have harmed yourself. And when you raise another to his highest, you have raised yourself. Think of all others as an extension of yourself. Another's hand is your hand. His heart is your heart. His soul is your soul. It is true. All are One. All must know the New Gospel: we are One.

Be One. Seek One. Act as One would act. This shall be your mantra. This is how you shall live your life. Be One. Seek One. Act as One would act. Cherish all as you cherish Me. Honor all as you honor Me. Praise all as you praise Me. Love all as you love Me. This is the way, for we are One. Each is the other and the other is you. Know this and honor this. Be One with all. It is the Way.

We know that you have come to us to find your way. Know that this is the Way. Know that you have come, and you are here. Do not worry about arriving; you are here already. Know that you are here, that you know All, and then live it. It is in the living that you will be All. There are no great secrets here. It is easy. Know All—live All—be All. It is the way Home. It is the way to Me. It is the way to You.

We know that you are ready. Your life has been many lifetimes waiting for this moment. You had to learn, and now you have. This is where the teachings have brought you. They have brought you to your knees. They have brought you to My feet.

February 2

We are Love and you are Love. Love is all there is. Know this and be still. We have come to give you a spiritual hug—a hug straight from God—a hug so that you know we love you. Feel us place our loving arms around you. Feel us gently squeeze you with our Love. This is a spiritual hug.

Hugging is the most effective way of communicating. Now you must know that some people will not appreciate this form of communication. Some are so closed that they do not wish another to enter their spiritual space. They are afraid of what others may see in their soul. Keep offering hugs. Never stop offering. Keep offering so that they will know that you are sincere. They do not trust, for they have been hurt. It is the hurt that keeps them at a distance. The distance will fade away and disappear when they know that they are worthy.

For those who are fearful, offer spiritual support in the form of a sincere word, a smile, or a handshake, but spiritual hugs are the nutrient of life. They are what the spiritually connected live for. Do not fear that you are not spiritually connected if you dislike or fear a hug. It is okay. All is just a lesson. All is learning. This is how it is meant to be for you. As time goes by, you may feel differently.

Do not worry about tomorrow. Live in the Eternal Now. Yesterday is gone, and tomorrow will take care of itself. Do not worry about those trivial things. Do not worry about anything. All is a lesson. All is in the learning. Do not look at a lesson as bad or wrong. All is just as it is meant to be in the continuous Circle of Life. You will learn, and you will complete the Circle. This is as it is to be.

Your world is learning, and one day all will be at the same place, and then the earth will be grand. Work toward that day, but do not expect that it will happen. It will happen when it is the right time. Do not wait for the right time, for it is in the waiting that all will not happen. Know that you already are spiritually connected both to the earth and to the Heavens. Know that you are, and it will be so. Create and it is as you created. This is the way of the earth to come. All shall create and know that all is exactly perfect. All shall be happy. All shall know that their Light is bright. This will be a glorious day on earth. Do not fear, for it is coming. The dawn is coming. Know that God is among you, and the world will be as it should be. Know that you are God—that you are walking among God—and you will have Heaven on earth. You will have peace and prosperity and love abounding. This is as it is to be.

February 4

You will know All when you remember All. This you must know. This you must believe. This has been the story for hundreds of centuries and will continue to be the story forever. There is no end to the Universe. The Universe is so big. It is bigger than any scientist will ever know. It encompasses all—all that can be seen, and all that cannot. Know this and believe.

There is so much more than you shall ever know as humans on earth. Your science could never explain the All that we know. There is more, so much more. There are beings that are Light. There are beings that are Love. These beings do not take the human form. There are many places to go when your new life begins. You can go here or you can go there or you can go everywhere. You can be All at the same time, for it is all happening at the same time in the Eternal Moment of Now. Now is all there is.

Your spirit is in many places. You are not only here, but you are there, and you are everywhere. Right now. Right now in the Eternal Moment of Now. Time is irrelevant. It is not here. The Universe is grander than anyone can imagine. Do not look for life on Mars or on Venus; it will not be there, not as you expect to find it. You are looking for human life. There is none elsewhere. Your planet is human life. Yours and only yours. There is no human life anywhere else, but there is life everywhere. Do not ever believe that there is not life on other planets and other stars and other moons and other places that you know not of. There is life everywhere.

There is life in every corner of the Universe. Stop looking and know. Tell the scientists to stop looking for proof of life, for they will not find it. For when you search for something, it is in the searching that your soul knows that you do not believe. But in the knowing, you know that it is there. The soul acknowledges this, and you see All. Tell all to stop searching, and just know. This is the key to All. Knowing and believing are the way to know All.

Save your money, for all the space searches will show nothing. Use the money saved to help all those who are in need—those who are in need of food, those who are in need of shelter, and those who are in need of medicine. Use your money for these things. Do not use it searching, for in the searching, you shall never find. You may as well throw the money into the sun and watch it burn to a crisp. Do not search—know. It is all there. It is all there right in front of your nose.

Do not ever think that you are the only intelligent life in the Universe. You are far from the most intelligent. You are the babies of the Universe. And babies sometimes have too much confidence. Know you are not the entire Universe. Know that you are the tiniest piece, the tiniest speck of dust. This is earth. Know that there is more. But know also that God loves each speck of dust, each crumb on the floor, and each piece of stone. God loves all, for God knows each speck of dust by its name. Know this and you will feel grand. For if God knows each speck of dust by name, He surely knows you. Know that God knows you by name, and you will feel as grand as that speck of dust. That speck is All. You are All. The Universe is All. Know this and be grand.

We have come to tell you these things so that you may know just how grand the Universe is. We are not telling you these things to make you feel small. No! Feel big and feel grand, for each is grand in his own being. But know that it is not only you who are grand, but all who are grand. Yours is not the only way. Yours is not the best way. Yours is *your* way. Feel proud of your way, but do not discount others' ways. Each has his way. Honor each and every way, for all are grand.

Remember: we are One. This is the New Gospel. We are One—and for that reason alone—we must love each other, we must respect each other, and we must share with each other. We must do this for all, even for the ones in the Universe that we do not think we know. Be One with all in the Universe, for it is in the being One with the Universe that you can be One with your Self. For you cannot be One with all others until you are One with your Self.

Love yourself. Honor yourself. Cherish yourself. Praise yourself. Then you will be able to love, honor, cherish, and praise all others, for you will know that you are they. And they are you. And we are them. And they are us. All are One. One continuous Circle of Life. Each is the other and the other is you.

February 7

We are Love and we are Light. To this be the end of all things. There is no end of all things. All things continue in the Circle of Love. All things are forever and forever. This is as it is to be. We come to you to tell you of all that is contained in the Divine Circle of Love. You are the Divinity. You are the one who puts the Divine into the

Circle. Each one of you is the Divine One. We have come to tell you of the grandness of you. We have come to tell you of the grandness of your world. We have come to tell you of the goodness that is you. We need to tell you all these things so that you believe and create your world to be all that it can be. Your world will be grand when you know that you can create. Create and know that you are grand.

This has been our story. This has been our song. You have come to us to hear our stories. You have come to us to hear the melodies that we sing. Know that you have received all that you have asked for. This will be the end for now. You have received all that you need for this moment. Go out into the world and live these messages. Do not worry that this is the end of our relationship; we will always be together.

Come to us when you are ready to learn more, and we will be there. There will be many more books to come, but know that you do not need these books. You know All already. It is in your soul. It is in your remembering. Know that you know, and you will know. Seek the Love. Seek the Light. Seek the Peace. Seek our Voices. Seek All and ye shall find. Take these words to heart and live them. Live them as you learn the lessons of your soul. This is the way to the All-in-All. This is the way to God. This is the way to knowing your Self. It is in the knowing of your Self that you will know God, for you are He and He is you. You are part of the Divine Circle. Know that you can never *not* be a part of the Circle. You *are* the Circle.

Know that we will always be waiting for you. Know that we will always be with you. Know that you are never alone. Know that today is yesterday and yesterday is tomorrow. All time is happening at once. Time does not exist. Know that you can be all places at once because it is all happening at once. Know that you shall live for today. This moment in time is the grandest moment of your life. This very moment. Live it to the fullest in Love.

Know that the world shall be saved, for all are learning. Take what you have learned here and be our messenger. Spread the New Gospel: we are One. Spread this Word to all who will listen. Spread this Word by living this Word. Live the New Gospel, and you will be our messenger. Live it so that all may see it. For it is in the seeing that all will believe.

This is your mission: be Peace. Be Peace to all. Be Peace to your enemies, for they know not what they do. Love thine enemies and hold them close. It is in the closeness of the Circle of Love that all fears shall melt. It is the fear that has made them your enemy. Melt the fears away with the Love in your heart. Be Peace to all. Show Peace to all. Be Peace. Seek Peace. Act as Peace would act.

Be a Light. Be a Light for all to follow. Shine your Light so that all may know the way. The Light is the Way. Your Light shall be a beacon for all to follow. Some will follow and some may not. Keep shining your beacon so all may follow when it is their time. Be Light. Seek Light. Act as Light would act. Your Light will not be alone. You shall never be alone. Your Light will be shining through our Light. It is grand. Know that it is grand, and it will be grand.

Love all for who they are at the moment. Do not judge. Do not condemn. Do not seek to change them. Love them for exactly who they are. It is their path. Honor the path that they are on. They are finding their way. Honor and cherish all, and you will know true Love. You will know the Love that God has given to you. Support all who are on their way. No matter where they are, they are on the path Home. Be with all, and you will know true Love. Love is all there is. Love shall conquer all things. Love is the answer. Love is the Way. Be Love and all will be just as it is meant to be. Love and support each and every person you meet. Honor their journeys even when they are on a different path than yours. Be with each soul as it journeys towards

Home. Be Love. Seek Love. Act as Love would act.

Be Kindness, for Kindness is Love. Show Kindness to all, and you shall enter their hearts. Kindness will break down the barriers of hate. Kindness will break down the barriers of doubt. Kindness will break down the barriers of fear. Kindness will bring out the Love. Be kind to all creatures, no matter how large or how small. Be kind even to the tiniest of flies, for he is God's most friendly creature. Be kind to all, and all shall be kind to you. Remember the Golden Rule: do unto others, as you would have them do unto you. It is the way to peace. Remember this and be still.

Remember that you are never alone. Ask and ye shall receive. We shall be with you always. God is with you always. I am with you always. Know that your soul shall never be alone. It is in the Love and in the Light that all the angels are held. Each soul holds these angels because each soul contains all the Love and all the Light. You do not have to search any farther than your own heart to find these things. All the Love and Light is there—right inside your heart. Know that they are there, and they will be there. Seek the Love and the Light, and they shall come from within and be there for all to see. Know that they are there, and they will be. Believe. Do not fear. Do not doubt. Do not expect. Know. Just know and just "be." This is the way. Know that you are us. Know that you are Him. Know that you are all the angels in Heaven. Know that you are God on earth.

Know that you are all these and more. You are more than the stars in the Heavens. You are more than the sun and the moon. You are more than the wind and the rain. You are more than the ocean and the sand. You are the Yin and the Yang. You are the Alpha and the Omega. You are the beginning and the end. You are God. Know this and you will know All.

Come to us, for we are waiting. Come to us, and let your soul fly. You are Love and you are Light. We love you.

Know this and you will be free. Free to fly with your soul. Free to be who you are. Free to let all be who they are. Come to us, and be free. Free yourself from the bondage of human life as you know it. Freedom is what you have been searching for. Be all these things, and you will be free. All will be Light. All will be Love. All will be Peace. Come. Be God. Be yourself. You are more your Self than you have ever been before.

Know this and be still.

It is all there within your heart.

Free your heart and come fly with us.

PART FOUR

Transforming

Anger into Forgiveness

&

Pain into Peace

If you knew Who walks beside you on the way
that you have chosen, fear would be impossible.

A Course In Miracles

Transforming

Anger into Forgiveness

& Pain into Peace

Remembering

My personal demons are hidden beneath layers of fat, and are so deeply embedded in my subconscious that they have become a part of me. Food is my protector, my lover, and my confidant. It is where I turn for comfort. It is where I turn to forget. Food has always been my drug of choice. The pain has been so well hidden that not even I knew it was there. It has only been through my reading, writing this book, and praying that I have become aware of the deep emotional scars which have been a part of me for most of my life.

Consciously, most of us feel that we effectively deal with life's tragedies. Everyone tells us to forget and move on, but forgetting is not always easy and so we need help. Food helped me forget. For you, it could be alcohol, drugs, sex, shopping, cleaning, smoking, coffee, work, or any other behavior or substance that makes your mind numb to the pain of remembering.

It is in the forgetting that the pain becomes buried deep in your subconscious. In time the pain may grow until it has become a part of you, and there it becomes your demon. To conquer this demon you must not forget, but remember. Remembering the pain is the only way to understand and learn. It is in the learning of the lesson that you will be able to easily let it go, allowing the anger to be transformed into forgiveness and the pain into peace.

However, when it comes to remembering, we are often our own worst enemy. We know somewhere deep inside that letting go of our anger will bring tremendous changes into our lives. We—as a body—do not always take kindly to change, opting rather to stay with the familiar. As much as we want to move out of the painful situation, a part of us is completely fearful because we do not know what our future will hold. If we stay where we are, we may be in pain, but at least we know what to expect!

With this conscious or unconscious fear of change firmly in place, our mind will do everything it can to protect us from the very shifts that would free us. We end up running our lives on auto-pilot creating each day just as the day before, instilling the same thoughts and fears into our mind until a continuous tape loop of imprisonment is established. This protection system of the mind leaves us trapped in a world truly of our own making, a world where we remain a victim.

Our story becomes so embedded into our daily life we forget that we could just remember and move forward at any time. Or perhaps you equate letting go with having to forgive. At times forgiving can seem almost impossible because sometimes what we have to forgive is—in our own minds—unforgivable. So like a dog with a bone, your mind will hang on to all the detailed horror stories of your life, thereby justifying all your anger and pain.

On the other hand the soul has nothing to fear, for it knows the pain is only a lesson in learning. It welcomes the pain. This the mind does not understand. It is full of fear and does not know why the soul would want to go through the pain, and so it tries to forget—all the while keeping the memories firmly implanted in the subconscious. The mind wants to protect the body and the soul, and so it thinks that

185

it is doing what is best.

The mind *thinks*—and this is where the problem begins. The mind thinks, but the soul *knows*. The soul knows the reason for each and every happening. It knows that every event and every person has been placed in your life—by *you*. It knows that in order to experience joy—it must first experience pain. It knows that it must experience sadness before it can recognize happiness, and loneliness before it can achieve Oneness.

Your soul knows that in order for you to know one thing, you must first experience the exact opposite. And truly, how would you know that it was a really cold day unless you had first experienced a really warm one? With this thought guiding you, perhaps you can see how you called all your experiences into your own life. We are all here experiencing what we have *asked* to experience. The people who have come into your life to hurt you and to worry you and to anger you were called here by you—so that you could experience remembering and letting go, which is just another way of saying, "find your peace."

When you try desperately to forget the pain, all you do is push these feelings deeper into your physical being. You have tried to deny it hoping that it will just go away, but to push it down means that you deny a part of yourself. Personal demons are nothing more than denied parts of you.

It is not in the forgetting that you will release your pain, but in the remembering and the embracing whatever it is as a part of your journey. Take the experience out and look at it fully. See it in the Light of God. See it through the Light of Love. Embrace the experience; do not deny it! Embrace it as a part of who you are. Embrace it as a part of your journey here on earth. See whatever the experience is as nothing more than a lesson in moving toward your Self, and ultimately, toward God.

It is time to rouse the demons that have been sleeping

peacefully. Awaken them, take them out, and look at them fully. Announce that they hold no power over you any longer. Release the pain. Release the fear. Release the doubts. Let them all go! What you look at fully will disappear.[5] It is time! The mind is ready to let the soul have its way.

Suggestions for Releasing Pain

❖ Pray.

❖ Have faith.

❖ Smile!

❖ Listen to joyful music.

❖ Forgive yourself!!!

❖ Make a list or audio tape of "I AM" affirmations and repeat or listen to them several times a day—affirmations such: as I am good, I am Love, I am Light, etc.

❖ When given a choice between pain and peace, choose whatever will bring you peace, disregarding the expected consequences.

---

[5] Neale Donald Walsch, *Conversations With God (an uncommon dialogue) - Book 1* (Hampton Roads Publishing Company, 1996) 100

❖ Light a candle, pray over the flame, and watch your prayers be taken directly to God.

❖ On a piece of paper, write down the painful experience and ignite the paper with a match. Watch as the smoke curls its way to God, taking all the pain along with it.

❖ Give up telling "your story" to yourself or to anyone else. Affirm to yourself: I am not a victim—I am Spirit!

❖ Erase the old negative tapes by visualizing a cassette tape inside your mind. First, listen to it and take note of which parts you want to keep and which you want to erase. Now imagine erasing all the parts that you no longer want to use to create your life. When the tape is erased, take out your affirmation list, hit the Record button, and make a new tape in your mind.

❖ Speak with love and forgiveness to the person who has hurt you. Even after someone has passed over, you can still release the pain because there is no end to life. The person will be with you as you speak to him or her.

❖ Meditate. Sit quietly and calm your mind. Think of the pain as a dark cloud. Imagine blowing the cloud away. As the cloud blows away, the pain is blown away also.

❖ Write in a journal, letting all the pain flow to the surface.

❖ Mentally send all the pain to the Light. Visualize the pain as a dark spot. Now see this spot moving through your body, out the top of your head, and to the Light where it will be cleansed.

❖ Give yourself lots of hugs!

❖ Try to see the humor in all things. Life is funny!

❖ Create peace within yourself by closing your eyes and visualizing a peaceful color within your mind. See this color filling every space of your mind, body, and soul— bringing peace to every area of your life.

❖ Go to the library and pick out a book that interests you—and actually take the time to read it.

❖ Make a "Joy Box." Get a small box and put things inside that make you happy, perhaps a feather, a crystal, etc. Along with these, put in slips of paper with joyful thoughts and ideas for creating joy written on them. Pull out some joy whenever you are in need.

❖ Exercise! Not only will your body feel better, but your mind will be clearer, too. Just start by taking a short walk and gradually add more time.

❖ Look in the mirror and tell yourself that you love every part of the person looking back at you. You could also do your "I AM" affirmations while looking in the mirror. Try this exercise without the benefit of clothes. Look at your body, and tell it that you love it just as it is. This is a wonderful way to create a healthy and strong body.

❖ Be helpful. Helping someone else will lift not only their spirits, but yours as well.

❖ Sing to God. Sing loudly, forcing all the pain out of your mouth and directly to God's ears.

❖ Be joyful. Pain wishes to stay with a mind that is hurting. When you are joyful, the pain will not wish to stay.

❖ Be loving. Be Love to all. Seek to see Love in all.

❖ Be truly thankful for the pain knowing that is the way to becoming whole once again. It is your way Home.

❖ Fake it 'til you make it. When you begin to implement these suggestions, they may feel like you are lying to yourself. Continue anyway. It may take some time, but eventually your mind will give up and actually begin to believe what you are telling it.

❖ Meditate upon the following questions:

- What do the words "let it go" really mean to me?
- Do they represent a conscious choice to change my life or are they just words that I say hoping that the choice and work will be magically taken out of my hands?
- What benefits am I getting out of holding on to my pain?
- What am I getting in return?
- What is staying in this pain allowing me to do or not to do in my life?
- Am I ready to give up my story?

- How would my life change if I didn't have this anger and pain?
- What would I lose if I allowed myself to forgive?
- What could I accomplish if I were to forgive everyone for everything?
- Do I love myself enough to give myself the gift of peace and forgiveness?

Call it forgiveness. Call it karma. Call it the path to peace or letting go. There is no moment that God is not with you. God was with you as He created you in His image and likeness. You are His Divine Creation. And God was there in your time of pain—holding your heart safe.

There is nothing that can be done with or to the physical body that can change your God-created Holiness. All you need to do is: remember … embrace … and what is not of God's Love—let go!

God is in every moment no matter who we are, where we are, what we are doing, or what is being done to us. God wants only happiness for his creations. God wants only joy for his children.

Remember …

and then let it go.

God will be there to take it from you.

Each of us carries the hurt of so many generations before us. Pain, anger, and fear are passed from grandparent to parent and finally to the child. It is no one's fault; there is no blame to be placed. There comes a time, however, when someone has to hold out his hand and say, "STOP!"

It is not until the merry-go-round of pain, abuse, and fear is stopped that you will be able to climb off. But when all you have known is the endless cycle of going round and round, jumping off this merry-go-round can seem impossible.

But ...

It is time.

It is time to summon all your courage and jump.

Jump to freedom.

Jump to a new life.

Jump into the arms of the Lord.

Know that He will be there to catch you.

Always and Forever.

Afterword

Seven New Year's Eve celebrations have come and gone since I felt the energy standing beside me. Governments have been overthrown, and we are once again at war. The proclaimed Axis of Evil, Saddam Hussein, has been executed, and I wonder whether we will ever collectively "get it."

However, as I reflect on my life's journey, I realize that my own feet have not always been on the path of forgiveness and peace. There appeared to be no hope for me either, and yet today, I have been transformed by those very footsteps.

Seven years ago I was broken—physically, mentally, and emotionally. On one of the days when the chemicals around me sent me crashing to the floor in an unconscious heap, the emergency room physician told me that I was essentially crazy. He may not have used that exact word, but his intention was clear. It was his attitude which sent me seeking for another way to heal. These messages became that other way, and I realize now how many blessings I have received throughout my seemingly arduous ordeal.

Today I am whole. Oh, there are still issues, both conscious and unconscious to be worked out, but I am whole—physically, mentally, emotionally, and spiritually. The voices of the angels still speak and I still listen, not every day, but when I need them, I know that they will always be there.

My journey led me to leave the teachings of my family church in search of my Higher Self. Through miracles disguised as serendipitous coincidences, my angel guides have choreographed each step in the dance of my life. All I had to do was to listen to the music and follow their lead.

193

Everything I needed to heal was provided for me. It is said that when the student is ready, the teacher will appear. My teacher, mentor, and guide appeared right on cue even though we had been acquaintances for several years. It was if she had just been waiting for me to "get it."

I am now an ordained nondenominational interfaith minister, and having been gifted the seeds for a new ministry by my mentor, Shelly and I started Celebrations of the Spirit. Presiding over our new "church" has lead me to finally be able to answer the question What do I want to be when I grow up? The answer to this question lay within my own heart. It is where all answers lie.

It has taken me seven years to adequately integrate these principals into my life, and to be able to clearly communicate what I believe to others. This book sat for the better part of six years, just waiting for the teacher in me to appear. Only then did I become consciously aware that I had fulfilled the tearful bargain made with God so many years ago. God *had* provided a path for my healing, and I had become a Messenger of His Word!

I am healed, whole, and healthy. It is what I have always been! The anger has been transformed into forgiveness and the pain into peace. It is all this which I offer to you now.

The world is not doomed no matter how bleak things may look. When the student is ready, the teacher *will* appear. In a leap of faith and a blaze of Light, you, and our world, will be transformed!

Melinda
January 2007

About the Author

Rev. Melinda A. Angstadt is a graduate of Circle of Miracles School of Ministry near Doylestown, Pennsylvania. She presides at Celebrations of the Spirit where her unique nondenominational interfaith Sunday services honor all religious traditions, spiritual paths and metaphysical sciences in an atmosphere of unconditional love.

As a Usui and Shamballa Reiki Master, she teaches individuals and groups the hands-on healing art of Reiki. She is also a student and a facilitator of A Course in Miracles.

Melinda makes her home in the beautiful farming community of Oley, Pennsylvania where she enjoys watching her gardens, her ministry, and her family grow.

ISBN 142511945-X

9 781425 119454